ESSAYS IN PETTO

ESSAYS IN PETTO

by

THE REV. MONTAGUE SUMMERS

Essay Index Reprint Series

BOOKS FOR LIBRARIES PRESS, INC.

FREEPORT, NEW YORK

FOR H. C. WHO SAYS HE LIKES
MY WORK

First published 1928
Reprinted 1967

PREFATORY NOTE

*I*T *sometimes happens at a consistory that the Holy Father, after creating certain cardinals, adds that he has nominated one or more additional cardinals, whom he reserves* in petto, *and whom he will make known later :* alios autem (hac uice duos) in pectore reseruamus, arbitrio nostro quandoque declarandos.

In collecting, for the first time—mainly on account of the frequently expressed wish of many friends, as also of many who have in their letters evinced no little interest in the themes I treat—a few of my Essays in a more permanent and accessible form, I have added two which until now were kept in pectore, *and these may serve in some sort to justify my title.*

Of the following papers one was written as far back as five-and-twenty years ago, and the youngest is fully fledged seven. It is certainly very gratifying to me that the subjects in which I was a pioneer should have attracted so wide attention. The Gothic romances, for instance, with which I was the first to deal in my essay on Ann Radcliffe, have since been studied in at least half-a-dozen academic theses ; none of these, however, proving (in my opinion) altogether satisfactory or authoritative. Moreover, novels from the Minerva Press and similar houses are to-day being sought for with no little assiduity, both in England and America, so that the works of Mrs. Roche, Mrs. Helme, Horseley Curties, and many another of their school, volumes of excessive rarity, now fetch high prices when they make infrequent appearance in the auction-room or the bookseller's catalogue. It may not be impertinent to mention that I have edited a re-issue of the seven " Horrid Novels " which are spoken of in Northanger Abbey, *and that I have for some years been engaged upon a somewhat detailed study of the Gothic romance and its influences.*

When I once more took them in hand I had the idea of revising these Essays of a decade and more ago, but upon actually re-reading them I realized that any adjustment of this kind must mean a re-writing of whole passages, alterations and amplifications which might well be considered illiberal and unfair. I agree with Huysmans : " Je pense que tous les gens de lettres sont comme moi, que jamais ils ne relisent leurs œuvres lorsqu'elles ont paru. Rien n'est, en effet, plus désenchantant, plus pénible, que de regarder, après des années, ses phrases." Nevertheless it is, I feel, more than doubtful whether one is at liberty to remodel and reform those phrases and expressions of thought. That one may, in certain exceptional circumstances, laudably reject and repudiate an earlier work I can understand. Whether for a re-issue one may honestly remould critical opinions is a nice question I do not feel called upon to decide. In any case let these Essays go forth as I originally penned them. It has seemed to me legitimate to correct an error here and there, a date maybe or an initial; but there is—I think—nothing essential that I would emend. I will merely premise that were I writing these papers now there might be some slight modification of expression—I would endeavour to praise Jane Austen more highly; I would be more generous in my appreciation of the sombre and sublime genius of Ann Radcliffe.

It only remains to add that the Essay upon Ann Radcliffe was (in an abbreviated form) delivered as a lecture to the Royal Society of Literature in January, 1917; that the Essay upon Jane Austen formed the Centenary Lecture addressed to the same Body; that the Essay on the Marquis de Sade was originally given in 1919 as a lecture to the British Society for the Study of Sex Psychology, when Mr. Laurence Housman took the chair; and that A Restoration Prompt-Book *is included by kind permission of the Editor of* The Times Literary Supplement, *where it first appeared.*

MONTAGUE SUMMERS.

CONTENTS

A GREAT MISTRESS OF ROMANCE:
ANN RADCLIFFE, 1764–1823

E.P.

A GREAT MISTRESS OF ROMANCE:
ANN RADCLIFFE, 1764—1823

THE macabre is a note which is to be found in a more or less marked degree—at certain periods almost wholly suppressed, and again at others unduly exaggerated—in all the literatures of the world. It is a subject which possesses an extraordinary power and fascination, a subject open to the most obvious dangers and trivialities. Informed by genius it reaches the grandest heights of shuddering tragedy; profaned by vulgar minds and cheap pens it grovels in the gutter an object of well-merited ridicule and disgust. It would be intensely interesting, if space allowed, briefly to indicate the existence and growth of this sentiment, which, adopting Pater's phrase, I have termed the macabre, this horror and awe, through the great literatures of all nations and times. This is impossible, but before approaching my main subject, the work of Mrs. Radcliffe, I would touch upon one or two points in classical Greek and Latin and in English literature where the supernatural and the awesome are markedly apparent.

It should be pointed out that there are two principal ways in which writers deal with the macabre. The object of both is, or ought to be, a serious effect—terror. The first method consists of an appeal to sheer physical dread and repulsion, by the description of and dwelling upon the black shadows of dissolution and decay, of mortal corruption, a brooding upon the gloomy and the sinister,

> "dismal preparation,
> [And] talk fit for a charnel."

Lafcadio Hearn, in an essay entitled "Nightmare-Touch," said that the fear of ghosts is the fear of being touched by ghosts, the dread of actual sensible contact with the supernatural—in one word, shock. Incidentally it may be remarked that Dr. Havelock Ellis tells us that Touch is of fundamental importance—

the skin is the Mother of all the other senses. On this essential idea is to a large extent based the first method of utilizing and dealing with the macabre in literature. This we find in many of Bandello's novelle, in the inhuman stories of Grazzini, in the *Orbecche* of Giraldi Cinthio, in Lewis' ghoulish romance *The Monk*, in the works of such a poet as Maurice Rollinat, and in much vulgar writing analogous to the *Police Times*.

But Hearn's explanation is only very partially true. The second method, far finer in its working and far keener in its result, is, without any emphasized and undue concentration upon what is merely ghastly and loathsome, to create an atmosphere, an intangible spiritual atmosphere of psychic dread, such as has been done with such consummate mastery and skill by the genius of Henry James in *The Turn of the Screw*, with such subtle terror by Mrs. Oliphant in her *Tales of the Unseen* and *The Beleaguered City*, with such terrific force by D'Annunzio in *La Città Morta*, by Van Lerberghe in *Les Flaireurs*, by Maeterlinck. In the very vagueness and uncertainty of such fear lies the terror ; there is a sense of some indefinable presence which may be able and about to manifest itself suddenly ; there is an utter inability to judge or cope with the extent of the power this presence can exercise, probably for evil and malignant ends. Sometimes the two methods are combined, as in Webster's magnificent tragedy *The Dutchesse Of Malfy*, where we find sepulchral properties such as the dead man's hand, a corpse brought to the murderer's room at midnight, poisoned books, coffins, cords, and a bell, waxen images counterfeiting death, where people can hardly say the simplest thing without some funereal metaphor, where they reproach each other in recklessly gruesome terms and talk of shrieking mandrakes, lycanthropy, disease, and yet with all these material affrightments Webster never oversteps the mark. The physically horrible touches are mere details on a far more terrible background of spiritual gloom and despair.

It has been rashly and mistakenly averred that in ancient Greek literature the macabre finds little place. And yet in the *Agamemnon* where we see the triumphant return of the king from Troy he brings with him the weird woman Cassandra, and, all others having passed into the house, she stands and shudders as she gazes upon the dazzling white walls of the palace rising calm and serene in the hot sunshine of the midsummer day. The

marble steps are covered with rich tapestries ; the statues of the
gods are garlanded with flowers ; all is joy, all is peace. The
chorus, the elders, watch her curiously, this barbarian captive.
And even as she hesitates the pangs of inspiration tear her.
She shrieks out that the phantom forms of murdered children,

"Whose hands are filled with meat of their own flesh,
Χεῖρας κρεῶν πλήθοντες οἰκείας βορᾶς,"

bleeding and woeful, crowd the house-roof. Hell and doom
are lurking within those festive doors. Slowly, painfully, fore-
knowing her own destruction, she approaches step by step,
keening as she goes. At the threshold she starts. The foul
smell of blood assails her. She shivers and recoils. " 'Tis but
the odour of the sacrifice upon the hearth," say the chorus.
" To me," rejoins the prophetess, " it is the reek of charnels."
But needs must. She touches the door and disappears. The
scene is empty. The chorus in low tones and disjointed speech
chant their terror and their dread. Anon there is silence.
And then suddenly the loud cry of Agamemnon rings out :
" Alas ! I am stricken with the stroke of death ! " It has been
said : " This shriek is the most terrible incident in all tragedy,
owing to its absolute and awful timeliness, its adequacy to the
situation." I have laid some little stress upon this catastrophe
owing to the manner in which Aeschylus creates his atmosphere.
I would emphasize, strongly emphasize, the romanticism of this
severely classic tragedian.

Other instances of the macabre might be cited from Greek
literature—the scene of the foul and hideous Furies slumbering
within the hallowed precincts of Delphi and the dark wraith of
Clytemnestra with the deep wound in her breast where the
blood is never staunched, rousing the avengers from their
sleep and hounding them on her son with bitter taunts and
biting tongue—the unearthly figure of Teiresias, the seer,
in the *Oedipus Tyrannus* and the terrible agony which closes
that tragedy—but enough has been said amply to show that
the macabre had its part in the most self-restrained of ancient
literatures.

Amongst Latin authors the macabre is strongly marked.
Both Horace and Lucan—who was imitated by the prolix
Silius Italicus—have descriptions of a witches' sabbat. With
no little irony Horace in his *Epistles* asks the man who piques

himself on being thoroughly unsentimental, unromantic, un-imaginative,

> " Somnia, terrores magicos, miracula, sagas,
> Nocturnos lemures, portentaque Thessala rides ? "

"Do you really laugh at dreams, magic spells, wonders, witches, the terror that walketh by night, and Thessalian prodigies ? " In Seneca's tragedies we have several apparitions. Particularly striking is the long description in *Oedipus* of the necromantic rites by which the spirit of Laius is evoked. In Propertius the ghost of Cynthia appears with crackling finger-joints,

> " Pollicibus fragiles increpuere manus,"

her robes are still scorched by the funeral pyre—" lateri uestis adusta fuit "—two very modern touches. At the immortal dinner of Trimalchio the guests tell each other ghost stories freely, and the host's hair stands on end—" si qua fides est pili inhorruerunt." But the most striking book where the romantic and macabre are combined is undoubtedly the *Metamorphoses* of Apuleius, a true decadent in language, style, and matter. At the outset Lucius confesses to an overwhelming interest in magic and occult arts. He is travelling in Thessaly, the very centre of wizardry and superstition, and indeed before long his curiosity affords him a drastic lesson in the craft of the warlocks and sorcerers. The episodes which deal with the supernatural, and they are many, are very powerfully told. Incidentally it is worth noting how completely the last book, XI, with its detailed and wonderful description of the mysteries of Isis, the processions, the ritual, the liturgy, contradicts Gautier's assertion that mysticism was unknown to the ancient world.

In the Middle Ages the supernatural and abnormal played a large part. It would indeed have been remarkable if a world which in the year 1000 reeled to its base, awaiting the crack of doom, which thrilled with the militant mysticism of the Crusades, which saw S. Bruno and his hermit Carthusians

> " come together for more loneliness,
> Whose bond is solitude, and silence all their part ; "

which suffered strange plagues and stranger ecstasies, should not in its literary expression have been most deeply imbued with the macabre. In the thirteenth century Rutebeuf's *Miracle de Theophile*, an ancestor of *Faust*, has scenes full of sinister and terrible import ; as also has the Coventry *Slaughter of the Innocents*. In the fifteenth century *Everyman* Death appears in person, grim and ghastly like Thanatos in the *Alcestis ;* and, above all, in the Towneley *Raising of Lazarus* there are macabre stanzas almost Websterian in their combination of loathsome detail and impressive restraint. In the Scottish alliterative poem *The Awntyrs of Arthur*, Guinevere's mother appears to her in the course of a hunt. The spectre is described in hideous wise. The body is black and gaunt, the eyes glow like live coals, a baleful toad sits and gnaws the skull. At the sight the hounds scatter in all directions, yelping wildly ; the birds rush through the trees in terror. In days, too, which witnessed the trials of Gilles de Rais, of Urbain Grandier, the bull of Innocent VIII, the witch discoveries of Bamberg, of Como, of Warboys in Huntingdonshire, of Pendle, men's minds were always prone to the abnormal, and the volumes of the demonologists, of Bodin, Delrio, the Franciscan Sinistrari d'Ameno, have pages as fantastic and macabre as anything in literature. I cannot refrain from quoting the little interlude, *The Three Queens and the Three Dead Men :*

1st Queen.	I am afeard.
2nd Queen.	Lo ! what I see ?
3rd Queen.	Me thinketh it be devils three !
1st Dead Body.	I was well fair.
2nd Dead Body.	Such shalt thou be.
3rd Dead Body.	For Godes love, be-ware by me !

It is hardly necessary even in passing to draw attention to the extraordinary popularity of the " Drama of Blood and Horror " in the Elizabethan theatre, inspired as it primarily was by the tragedy of Seneca and his lurid Italian imitators, but which soon utterly cast aside the stiff trappings of formal classicism to take a completely native dress and tongue, to deal with actual events and recent crimes such as the murder of the Kentish squireen Arden ; the madness and infanticides of Walter Calverly ; the clubbing to death of Robert Beech and his boy by a dissolute tavern-keeper, Thomas Merry ; the execution of Mistress Browne and her servant at Bury St. Edmunds. It is interesting to know that Kyd's *Spanish Tragedy* was attracting audiences as late as 1668 ; and *Titus Andronicus* proved a great favourite in the first decade of Charles II's reign. In the winter of 1686, when Shakespeare's play was revived after an interval of some ten years, Ravenscroft, in order to make it more palatable, added a few additional murders and sundry ferociously horrible speeches and torturings.[1] Even in the sober reign of George II Lillo, the most moral and sentimental of all dramatists, was drawing upon old Elizabethan ballads and chapbooks for his great successes, *The London Merchant*, *Fatal Curiosity*, and *Arden of Feversham*, which last is merely an alteration of the older tragedy.

These things belong to the cruder presentation of the macabre, to that order which is physically horrible and revolting even, rather than to the terrible, the atmosphere of spiritual dread. But the latter is by no means untouched. We find it in Webster, in Ford, in Marston, in Cyril Tourneur, in the melancholy fantasies, the Nocturnals and Obsequies of Donne, a poet in whose praise I find it difficult to speak with words on this side idolatry. Nor can I neglect to mention the last sermon preached by the Carolan dean of S. Paul's, delivered at Whitehall in Lent, 1630, before the King, a sermon whose sonorous periods—as Sir Edmund Gosse has admirably said—" are adorned with fine similes and gorgeous words as the funeral trappings of a king might be with gold lace. The dying poet shrinks from no physical horror and no ghostly terror of the great crisis which he was himself to be the first to pass through . . . our blood seems to turn chilly in our veins as we read." When published in 1632 the book presented an extraordinary frontispiece, the head and bust of a corpse wrapped in a winding sheet. The poet as he lay on his death-bed had the ghastly fantasy to be placed in a coffin and to be drawn in his shroud.

Swinburne half hints that on the stage Cyril Tourneur makes too much play with skulls and crossbones, yet I cannot but think that the churchyard scenes of *The Atheist's Tragedy* are entirely justified both from a poetic and a dramatic standpoint. In such a play as the *Death's Jest Book* of Beddoes, a poet who " dedicated himself to the service of death," no doubt the macabre element would not bear presentation. The midnight feast of bleaching atomies and their partners, the dance to

---

[1] Quin, who played Aaron in the eighteenth century, was famous in this rôle. Ira Aldridge, the " negro tragedian," acted Aaron in London during his last engagement there, 1865. When *Titus Andronicus* was revived at the " Old Vic " in October, 1923, George Hayes gave a performance of Aaron, instinct with genius, in this magnificent, if terrible, drama.

rattling music, whilst a sentinel skeleton armed with a scythe sings a hideous song, these are too grotesque ; they would defy the producer's skill. Sir Edmund Gosse (who in an illuminating passage compares Beddoes in poetry to Breughel in painting) writes again that Beddoes " followed the very tricks of Marston and Cyril Tourneur like a devoted disciple." I would even venture to add that he caricatured them. I trust my above criticism will not be thought impertinent because Beddoes wrote with no idea of the stage. *Death's Jest Book* is a play, and as such it is, I think, legitimate to discuss it from the producer's point of view. A churchyard may be presented with great effect. *Hamlet* will, of course, occur to every mind. Very impressive is the final scene of Wedekind's *Frühling's Erwachen*, where, on a clear November night in the bright frosty moonshine, Melchior, escaping from the reformatory, clambers across the wall and encounters his chum, the suicide Moritz Stiefel, who comes stamping over the graves with his head under his arm, whilst presently the talk between the two boys, the quick and the dead, is interrupted by the mysterious figure of " Der vermummte Herr."

Terrible, too, is the last act of Laparra's *La Habanera*, which shows us ancient vaults and a campo santo wherein grow tall cypress trees like burned-out torches, dark against the faded sky. Pilar and Ramon are kneeling by the tomb of the murdered Pedro, and as the sun sets and the shadows grow deeper she flings herself into his arms with words of love, words which are drowned in the mournful chant of a belated funeral *cortège*, " Ego sum resurrectio et uita," a chant repeated again and again. She falls back crooning the dance music of la habanera, music which becomes mute before the booming of the solemn dirge. And then in horror, leaving her motionless, inert, Ramon flies, and the last sound we hear is the iron clang of the cemetery gate.

These are modern examples of tragedy, and it was tragedy that preserved the macabre from utter forgetfulness in the long period of 100 years from the Restoration to the beginning of the reign of George III. It is most noticeable how absolutely matter-of-fact, business-like, and entirely untouched by the shadow of the ghostly is such a relation as the narrative of " The Apparition of one Mrs. *Veal*, the next day after her death, to one Mrs. *Bargrave*, at *Canterbury*, the eighth of *September*, 1705," surely one of the most designedly plain and commonplace, as it is one of the cleverest, pamphlets in our literature.

It is pretty generally held that Horace Walpole was the first to introduce us to prose romanticism in 1764, and it may be allowed that *The Castle of Otranto* is the first piece of romantic fiction to make its influence widely felt, to be copied and advertised as the pioneer of a fashion and a school. None the less, Walpole was not the earliest of our prose romanticists, a position repeatedly but erroneously claimed for him. Two years before *The Castle of Otranto* appeared was published *Longsword, Earl of Salisbury*, " An Historical Romance," which is to be attributed to the Rev. Thomas Leland, D.D., of Dublin (1722–85), an Irish historian and classical scholar of repute. The work is picturesque, but on the whole poorly executed. Yet it certainly is the first English romantic novel, and although *Otranto* is famous and *Longsword* has been wholly forgotten, although *to* Walpole is—not undeservedly—ascribed far-reaching influence, and to Leland apparently little or none, yet the name of the latter should not have been so entirely obliterated from the history of fiction as in the past. Undeniably he is the first of our romantic novelists, and as such should be given his place and due.

But the fact that tragedy had paved the way and preserved the romantic spirit must not be minimized nor overlooked. Nor should that most powerful tragedy of Walpole's own, which Scott judged to be " horribly impressive "—*The Mysterious Mother*—be disregarded in this connexion. Yet what was the heroic theatre of Dryden save drama of a highly romantic order and the finest quality ? *Don Sebastian, Venice Preserv'd, The Mourning Bride*, Thomson's *Tancred and Sigismunda*, all carried on the same tradition and partook of the same spirit ; whilst Home's *Douglas* (produced at Covent Garden in March, 1757, and in Edinburgh the December of the preceding year) from the very first lines—

> " Ye woods and wilds, whose melancholy gloom
> Accords with my soul's sadness, and draws forth
> The voice of sorrow from my bursting heart . . ."

to the close of the fifth act—

> " Let every rite
> With cost and pomp upon their funerals wait,"

is surely romanticism *in excelsis*.

I do not say that tragedy was the only form of literature which preserved romanticism alive. That would be altogether too sweeping when we remember the odes of Collins ; the pinchbeck fantasies of Macpherson, received with enthusiasm they little deserved ; the work of Joseph and Thomas Warton ; and in later years, that isolated classic, *Vathek*, which owed nothing to current tendencies of thought. But tragedy, I repeat, was the main channel of romanticism.

With all its faults, its absurdities if one will—and they are many—*The Castle of Otranto* must ever have, for me at least, its own rococo fascination. It is a romance I prefer to enjoy rather than to defend, and in spite of the fact that the mammoth members and giant armour of Alphonso seen in the courtyard and in several chambers of the castle, the statue that bleeds from the nose, the picture walking out of its panel on the wall, and the many swarming wonders ere long make us feel, like Manfred himself, " inured to the supernatural," none the less, with every reservation, I am prepared to acknowledge that I find Walpole's pages never lose their charm, albeit 'tis but the memory of a fragrance long since faded. Perhaps, indeed, the spell in part consists of their utter remoteness from anything of to-day. I think no critic has remarked the extreme appositeness of the introduction of the name of S. Nicholas, which Gray seems to have found more incredible than any other of the wildest incidents in the story. Otranto lies at no great distance from Bari, the headquarters of the cult of S. Nicholas, who is indeed popular throughout the South-east coast of Italy. Nowadays the pother of the first preface of *The Castle of Otranto* with its talk of a book " printed at Naples, in the black letter, in the year 1529," of Onuphrio Muralto and William Marshall, can but provoke a smile, an unfortunate prelude to a tale of horror. Walpole's servants are hardly happy in their prolixity, and Mrs. Radcliffe was presently to show how the type of the garrulous domestic, faithful but a very magpie, could be used with far greater skill. The figure itself is, of course, from comedy. Dryden was one of the first to exploit it, and his Maskall in *An Evening's Love* and Benito in *The Assignation* yet hold their own. They are in some sense derived from the Spanish theatre of Lope de Vega, Juan Perez de Montalvan, and Calderon. Even in so mystic and sombre a tragedy as *La Devocion de la Cruz*, or in so philosophical a drama as *La Vida es Sueño* the *gracioso* has no insignificant place.   In comedy he is rampant.

Walpole soon found a disciple.   In 1777 Clara Reeve, the estimable daughter of a respectable clergyman, published *The Champion of Virtue*, " a picture of Gothic Times and Manners," a story which the authoress herself informs us is the " literary offspring of *The Castle of Otranto.*"   A second edition, called for in 1778, was dubbed *The Old English Baron*, under which name the book is now generally known.   Miss Reeve, however, was far from approving of the violence of Walpole's supernatural machinery, and although she admits a phantom he must needs behave soberly and decorously as a discreet and gentlemanly ghost should.   The result is that her work is cold and common-place enough ;   Walpole himself damned it as a *caput mortuum*, and sarcastically remarked it was indeed " *Otranto* reduced to reason and probability."   Clara Reeve failed egregiously, but she probably died quite unconscious of her failure.   Her name is more than partially forgotten, and has been almost wholly obscured by her far greater successor, Ann Radcliffe.

The life of Mrs. Radcliffe need not detain us long.   It was, in truth, so very quiet and domestic, so entirely without incident, that when Christina Rossetti wished to write the biography of the great queen of romance, whom she immensely admired, she was obliged to relinquish her project owing to lack of material.

Ann Radcliffe, born in London,[1] July 9th, 1764, was the only daughter of William and Ann Ward.   The father, though in trade, was a nephew of William Cheselden, the famous surgeon ; and her mother, whose maiden name was Oates, was first cousin to Sir Richard Jebb, physician to George III.   Her parents being in very comfortable and easy circumstances, a great part of Ann Ward's youth was spent with her superior relations, with whom she seems to have been a prime favourite.   She was in particular a frequent guest at the house of the partner of Josiah Wedgwood, Bentley, who had married her aunt, and who resided first at Chelsea and afterwards at Turnham Green. Here she met several of the chief literary and social figures of the day, amongst others, Mrs. Thrale, whose intimacy with Dr. Johnson had begun in the winter of 1764, and who was to

---

[1] In the parish of S. Andrew's, Holborn, where it was once fabled John Webster had been sexton and clerk.

marry Gabriele Piozzi in 1784 ; the famous Mrs. Montagu, the blue-stocking ; Mrs. Ord ; and James Stuart, " Athenian Stuart," a pioneer of classical archæology. Mr. Bentley's shy little niece seems to have attracted considerable attention both from her beauty of person and charm of manner. One day William Radcliffe, an Oxonian, and a student of law, who later abandoned being called to the Bar and became proprietor and editor of the *English Chronicle*, fell in love with this modest girl whose heart and hand he soon won. They were married at Bath in 1787, and it may here be remarked that Mrs. Radcliffe's wedded life was one of unclouded happiness, cheered by the devotion and admiration of her husband, who has left on record his deep affection for his amiable partner.

William Radcliffe's business often keeping him out late at night, and her own household tasks and cares over, the young bride sat down to pass the time by penning a tale. It is said that her husband urged her to make the attempt, and it was on those long solitary winter evenings spent in a quiet room by a blazing fire that she wrote the strange and romantic stories which, with all their faults, so unmistakably bear the hall-mark of genius. She composed rapidly, and the effects of this haste are now and again discernible in some details of her work, some incident is left unexplained, some promised solution of an event is forgotten, some thread not gathered up. It is, I think, obvious that she as thoroughly enjoyed telling her stories as we do reading them.

Her first romance, *The Castles of Athlin and Dunbayne, A Highland Story*, printed in 1789, is of no great length, and it must be regarded merely as an essay, a first step. It is a wild tale with improbable and strained incidents, often disconnected and confused, yet it appears to have met with considerable success. It ran into several editions, and in 1824 attained to the honour of being " embellished with engravings," to wit, two full-page woodcuts in the style of Pollock's juvenile theatre. 1836 is the date of the last separate edition I have examined, and although there may be even a more recent reprint, I do not think it was well known after the middle of the last century. To-day, I imagine, it is almost entirely unread. On May 9th, 1806, there was produced at Covent Garden, for the benefit of Miss Smith, a tragedy by George Manners entitled *Edgar, or Caledonian Feuds*, professedly founded on Mrs. Radcliffe's novel. It is a poor drama, and won scant favour. *The Castles of Athlin and Dun-bayne* was translated into French and published in Paris, 2 vols., 1819. There is, of course, no effort in this " Highland story " to describe either the manners or scenery of Scotland, but the discerning critic will notice, and, if he be generous, admire, a feeling for nature, a power of imagery which give speedy promise of finer things.

To a very marked extent this promise was fulfilled in *The Sicilian Romance*, published in 1790, a notable advance upon its predecessor. The book met with great success, and was avidly read even in the highest quarters. Already has Mrs. Radcliffe won her title of " the first poetess of romantic fiction." The opening which describes a traveller halting before the sombre and decaying ruins of the castle of Mazzini is a fine piece of word-painting pregnant with impressive suggestion. Anon he obtains hospitality at a neighbouring monastery, where he is allowed access to the library, and from an ancient manuscript extracts the story of the deserted walls. The stern Marquis of Mazzini, who has newly married a second wife, would force his daughter Julia, who loves the Count de Vereza, to wed the Duke of Luovo. Much of the book is taken up with Julia's flight from her father. She is captured and brought back, but escapes once more. Mystery surrounds the castle. In the deserted rooms doors are heard to close at night, and now and again there is " a sullen groan." These noises prove to proceed from none other than Mazzini's first wife, who is not dead, as supposed, but imprisoned by him in secret chambers. Eventually Mazzini's second lady, who has been faithless, poisons him and stabs herself. Julia and her lover are united, and all retire to Naples, leaving the castle to solitude and ruin. A very powerful use does Mrs. Radcliffe make of subterraneous passages, trap-doors with flights of steps descending into darkness, gothic windows that exclude the light, the sobbing of the wind, the wild haunts of Sicilian banditti. One incident in particular has been remem-bered by novelists and painters not a few. The Duke of Luovo, in pursuit of Julia, at nightfall finds himself near a distant monastery. On knocking at the door the porter refuses him admittance, alleging that the inmates are at their devotions and may not be disturbed. The Duke, after some parley, enters by force, and finds a company of jolly, well-paunched friars presided over by a rosy superior feasting in the refectory.

There have been innumerable editions of *The Sicilian Romance*. Only a few years ago it was issued in some sixpenny series. It has been translated into French more than once, and in Italy it is especially popular. In 1883 Simonetti of Milan published at a lira a translation with woodcuts, which are far from despicable, *I Sotterranei di Mazzini*. In 1889 Sonzogno of Milan printed quite a new version as *Giulia, o i Sotterranei di Mazzini* in the "Biblioteca Romantica Tascabile," at 50 centesimi. Myself I confess I always re-read *The Sicilian Romance* with considerable pleasure.

The Romance of the Forest, which appeared in 1791, is a far better planned and regulated work. The characters, too, especially the vacillating La Motte, weak but not criminal, and his wife, are distinct and well sustained. From the very first sentence interest is awakened—the hurried midnight flight of La Motte from Paris, the extraordinary way in which the heroine, Adeline, is entrusted to him, the romantic forest and ruined abbey where he takes shelter, his fears for discovery, his clandestine visits to the tomb, the deep-laid plots of the unscrupulous Marquis de Montalt, all are described in the most interesting way. The book is certainly romantic rather than macabre ; in fact, the supernatural plays a very small part, although the mysterious is by no means wanting. Extremely beautiful is Mrs. Radcliffe's description of the luxuriant woods, the huge-girthed oaks, the avenues and far-stretching vistas, the cool stream winding past the grassy lawns, the gothic abbey, a vast pile, lone and deserted now, but bearing traces of ancient grandeur and wealth.

James Boaden, the clever biographer of Kemble, Mrs. Siddons, Mrs. Jordan, and a playwright of no mean capacity, dramatized *The Romance of the Forest* as *Fontainville Forest*. *Fontainville Forest*, produced at Covent Garden on March 25th, 1794, was received with much favour. It was frequently acted the first season to crowded houses. The play follows the romance pretty closely, and is, it must be confessed, a skilful enough piece of work. Pope created La Motte ; Mrs. Pope, who had acted Cordelia to Garrick's Lear, Adeline ; Farren, the Marquis ; and Hull, Peter, a comic servant. With some slight alterations, the piece was revived at the same theatre January 8th, 1796, and, it was found, had lost nothing of its popularity.

So great a success was *The Romance of the Forest* that Messrs.

Robinson offered Mrs. Radcliffe £500 for her next novel; a sum then so unusually large for a work of fiction that Cadell, the famous publisher, on hearing the statement, wagered five guineas it was a mere canard. *The Mysteries of Udolpho* appeared in the spring of 1794, and at once exceeded even the warmest expectations. It straightway became, and has since remained, the most popular of her writings, and the very title passed into a proverb in our language. "The public," it has been said, "rushed on it with the most eager curiosity and rose from it with unsated appetite." Edition after edition was called for and rapidly exhausted. Joseph Warton, then Headmaster of Winchester, happening to take it up one evening, found it impossible to go to bed till he had finished the book, and sat up the greater part of the night for that purpose. Sheridan and Fox both speak of it in terms of the highest praise. Indeed, judged as a pure romance, it must be accorded a prominent place in fiction. It is a book which it is impossible to read and forget. The description of Udolpho is written with consummate power and skill—those dark battlements, high amid the Apennines, a castle of awe and gloom, through whose halls and shadowed corridors prowl armed bandits, at whose evil banquets the Venetian glass cracks as the poisoned wine hisses into it poured from the host's hand, in whose inmost chambers are hidden horrors not to be guessed at nor named. Not only do strange and unwonted sounds appal us, but the rushing wind, a rustling curtain, a half-heard sigh, the lonely watch-word on the terrace are startling and eerie here.

In 1797 was published in Paris a French translation of *The Mysteries of Udolpho* from the pen of Victorine de Chastenay, a well-known woman of letters of the day. This was frequently reprinted. There is one specially noticeable edition of 1808, in six duodecimo volumes, each of which has an exquisite frontispiece. These are none the less delightful because—although the period of *The Mysteries of Udolpho* is 1584, the reign of Henri III—in these illustrations all the characters wear the costumes of the directoire, and the ladies are robed and coiffed *à la grecque*. On the 19 Frimaire year VII—December 9th, 1799—there was produced at the Ambigu-Comique a spectacular drama by Réné-Charles Guilbert de Pixérécourt entitled *Le Château des Apennins, ou le Fantôme Vivant*, entirely founded on *The Mysteries of Udolpho*. Pixérécourt, who died in 1844, was an experienced writer, his plays, of which nearly two hundred are known, almost rivalling in number the prolific Lope de Vega. He had done his work cleverly, and the new melodrama thronged the theatre.[1]

In the summer of 1794 Mrs. Radcliffe accompanied her husband on a tour through Holland and the western frontier of Germany, returning down the Rhine. The same year she stayed in the lake district of Westmorland, and she has recorded her impression of these two visits in a well-written work entitled *A Journey . . . through Holland*, 4to, 1795.

The Italian, which was published in 1797, and for which Robinson gave £800, has far more unity of plan than *The Mysteries of Udolpho*, and is, in my judgment, the finest of Mrs. Radcliffe's works. The wooing of Ellena by Vivaldi, wooing overshadowed by the dark and mysterious figure of Schedoni, a masterly study in psychology, and as such the unifying *motif* of the book; the machinations of the monk and the Marchesa for the murder of the heroine; her capture and confinement in the convent among the hills, a landscape most beautifully described; her terrible sojourn with Schedoni in the fisherman's hovel by the sea when her lover has been seized by the familiars of the Holy Office; the awful conversation with the ruffian when the deed is planned; the long and hideous preparations as Schedoni mans himself to strike the blow; his strange relentings and bitter remorse; the episodes in the dungeons of the Inquisition when fear of bodily torture is almost overcome by apprehension of the supernatural; these are all scenes depicted in the most impressive and romantic manner, scenes in which the genius of the authoress shows itself capable of a power and an eloquence which till then perhaps had hardly been realized. The descriptive passages, and they are many, have been compared to the style of Salvator Rosa. That there are occasional inaccuracies, absurdities even, in this, as indeed in all of Mrs. Radcliffe's works, will hardly disturb the candid critic. In *The Castles of Athlin and Dunbayne* a lover indites sonnets of sixteen and twenty

---

[1] The first French play taken from *The Mysteries of Udolpho* was Alexandre Duval's *Montoni, ou le Château d'Udolphe*, produced at the Théâtre de la Cité, 29 July, 1798. In spite of the title, *Le Testament, ou les Mystères d'Udolphe*, of Lamartelière, produced a few weeks earlier at the Théâtre Louvois, borrows but one incident from Mrs. Radcliffe's romance according to the author, who has, however, not hesitated to adopt her remote castle and echoing corridors; her garrulous servants; her atmosphere of terror and suspense.

lines ; in *The Mysteries of Udolpho* there is talk about the opera as a fashionable amusement at Toulouse in the days of the League ; in *The Italian* a Carmelite nun is clad in "white drapery " ; an abbess appears with a mitre on her head ; the vesper-bell rings for mass, which is celebrated in the evening. But these and other such errors can, I think, be honestly condoned. A more vulnerable point of criticism is that until her last and posthumous work, *Gaston de Blondeville*, Mrs. Radcliffe refrained from the use of supernatural machinery, and at the close of her romances explains by natural agency the whole marvels of her story. Frequently the cause is totally inadequate to the effect, and we are obliged to confess a serious blemish here. In this connexion the words of the *Quarterly Review* for May, 1810, a just, if drastic, passage, can be cited and confirmed : "We disapprove of the mode introduced by Mrs. Radcliffe, and followed by Mr. Murphy and her other imitators, of winding up their story with a solution, by which all the incidents appearing to partake of the mystic and marvellous are resolved by very simple and natural causes. . . . We can believe, for example, in Macbeth's witches, and tremble at their spells ; but had we been informed, at the conclusion of the piece, that they were only three of his wife's chambermaids disguised for the purpose of imposing on the Thane's credulity, it would have added little to the credibility of the story, and entirely deprived it of its interest."

The masterly way in which Mrs. Radcliffe has made use of the Inquisition, and the restraint which she has exercised in depicting the scenes in the cells and sombre halls of that tribunal, are most noticeable. The Inquisition itself has, of course, been employed in many subsequent novels, but never with such decorum and effect.

Immediately upon its appearance *The Italian* was translated into French by no less a personage than the Abbé André Morellet.[1] Boaden dramatized Mrs. Radcliffe's chapters, and August 15th, 1797, there was produced at the Haymarket *The Italian Monk*, a play which is partly written in prose and partly in blank verse. The adaptor has made several changes, and supplied a happy ending. Schedoni was created by Palmer, the original Joseph Surface ; Vivaldi, Charles Kemble ; Paullo, Dicky Suett, of

[1] *L'Italien, ou le Confessional des Pénitents Noirs*, Paris, Denné, 3 vols., 12mo. 1797 ; and 4 vols., 18mo, 1797.

shambling gait and slippery tongue; Ellena, Miss de Camp. The first season it was acted twelve times, and it was revived in the following year at the same house for Miss de Camp's benefit on May 30th.

The Italian was the last of Mrs. Radcliffe's works to be published in her lifetime, and from 1797 till her death she withdrew herself in a more than ordinary privacy of domestic life, entirely declining to be lionized and *fêted* by London society. Scott, no doubt correctly, assigns as her motive for this exceptional and even rigid seclusion a disgust " at seeing the mode of composition which she had brought into fashion profaned by the host of servile imitators, who could only copy and render more prominent her defects, without aspiring to her merits." As the years passed by in silence various rumours began to circulate. It was suggested that she was travelling in Italy, a country she never visited, and there accumulating material for new romances. A pamphleteer was at some pains to describe her methods of composition, and told a gulled public how she was wont to sup late on underdone pork chops to induce nightmare, which was her inspiration. Often it was openly asserted and confidently believed that she was dead; obituary notices appeared. Another yet more persistent report stated that through brooding over horrors and terror a deep melancholia had invested her, and this had increased to such an extent that tottering reason gave way and she was perforce confined in a private asylum. A minor poet of the time rushed into print with an " Ode to Mrs. Radcliffe on her lunacy." She did not even give herself the trouble to contradict what people were saying. The only time she expressed annoyance and concern was when Miss Seward, in a letter dated May, 1799, stated how literary gossips were hinting that Joanna Baillie's *Plays on the Passions*, published the previous year, belonged to Mrs. Radcliffe's pen and that she was quietly owning them.

For several reasons it was Mrs. Radcliffe's custom to take excursions with her husband through beautiful and interesting parts of England. Thus they thoroughly explored the southern coast and much of the midland counties. But during the last twelve years of her life she at intervals suffered greatly from spasmodic asthma, which considerably affected her general health and spirits. On January 9th, 1823, a violent attack of the disease seized her. After a serious turn she appeared to rally, but being exceedingly weak, she died quietly in her sleep between two and three in the morning on February 7th. She was in the fifty-ninth year of her age. Her remains were interred in a vault in the Chapel of Ease, Bayswater, belonging to St. George's, Hanover Square.

Her husband, who survived her many years, in 1833 published, or rather edited, four volumes of her posthumous works. These included *Gaston de Blondeville*, a romance; *St. Albans Abbey*, a metrical tale; and various poetical pieces. Other poetical works also appeared separately. Of Mrs. Radcliffe's verse it is not necessary to say much. It is graceful and facile enough *St. Albans Abbey* itself, an imitation of *Marmion* and *The Lay of the Last Minstrel*, gives some happy lines, which we might esteem more highly were it not for Scott's originals. *Gaston de Blonde-ville*, feigned to be taken from an old manuscript, has the scene laid at Kenilworth Castle, and deals with the " Court of Henry III keeping festival in Arden." It is rather curiously divided into " eight days " [eight parts or chapters]. The influence of Scott can be very clearly detected, and Mrs. Radcliffe is far from her best here. There seems also a certain languor in the narrative, as though it had been written with effort which had not quite succeeded.

It is often said that Jane Austen, the most perfect, if not the greatest, of English novelists, began *Northanger Abbey* as a satire on Mrs. Radcliffe. This is only very partially true. *Northanger Abbey* is a satire, gentle and delicate enough, not on Mrs. Rad-cliffe, whose work is therein mentioned in terms of warm and sincere admiration, but on the school of Mrs. Radcliffe, that legion of imitators who distorted and caricatured the romance and genius of Udolpho—a very different story. This important distinction has, I think, rarely, if ever, been recognized and emphasized by the critics. George Mathias also in a note to the First Dialogue of his satire, *The Pursuits of Literature* (1811), when he writes contemptuously of the whole tribe of female novelists, especially excludes Mrs. Radcliffe from his censure. He says : " Mrs. Charlotte Smith, Mrs. Inchbald, Mrs. Mary Robinson, Mrs. etc., etc., though all of them are very ingenious ladies, yet they are too frequently *whining* or *frisking* in novels, till our girls' heads turn wild with impossible adventures." He then continues : " Not so the mighty magician of *The Mysteries of Udolpho*, bred and nourished by the Florentine muses in their secret solitary caverns, amid the paler shrines of Gothic superstition and in all the dreariness of enchantment; a poetess whom Ariosto would with rapture have acknowledged as

'La nutrita
Damigella Trivulzia al Sacro Speco.' "

In *Northanger Abbey* it will be remembered that Miss Andrews, " a sweet girl, one of the sweetest creatures in the world," recommended Isabella Thorpe some seven novels, which, " having read every one of them," she vouched as being " horrid." And now, one hundred years after, I have to thank Miss Andrews for her list. Following her good example, " having read every one of them," I thoroughly endorse her opinion, " horrid " being transmuted to " exciting." They are all, it may be mentioned, of an excessive rarity. In their day they were borrowed from the circulating libraries and read and read, until they were literally read to pieces. The list is as follows : *Castle of Wolfenbach, Clermont, Mysterious Warnings,*[1] *Necromancer of the Black Forest, Midnight Bell, Orphan of the Rhine,* and *Horrid Mysteries.* It has even been surmised that some of these titles are false, the invention of Jane Austen herself. But no, they are all genuine, and all actually exist. A few details may be of interest. *The Castle of Wolfenbach, A German Story,* first published in 1793, is by Mrs. Eliza Parsons, a most prolific novelist, who died in 1811. She was the daughter of a Plymouth wine merchant named Phelp. For some time she resided near Bow Bridge, and on the occasion of a dreadful fire by her presence of mind she saved, it is said, the whole of Bow from destruction. For this service she was granted a small place at Court. *The Castle of Wolfenbach* was reprinted as late as 1835. Hers also is *The Mysterious Warning*, which bears the date 1796. *Clermont*, by Regina Maria Roche, was first published in 1798, and translated into French by Victorine de Chastenay. Mrs. Roche, who died in 1845, was Irish, and is of course a fairly well-known writer. Her *Children of the Abbey* was frequently reprinted ; and I possess editions of 1854 and 1865. She inclines to sentimentalism rather than sensationalism. *The Necromancer ; or, The Tale of the Black Forest*, 2 vols. (1794), a product of the

---

[1] This should be *The Mysterious Warning ;* the title as given in *Northanger Abbey* is incorrect.

Minerva Press, purports to be "translated from the German of Lawrence Flammenburg by Peter Teuthold." Lawrence Flammenburg is the pseudonym of K. F. Kahlert, and Teuthold, no doubt, was one of the many literary Germans living in London at that time. This novel is peculiar in that following Mrs. Radcliffe the author explains all his ghostly visions and mysterious phenomena by natural means. The Necromancer is a charlatan and a cheat; the spectres a band of robbers, who at the conclusion are decimated and dispersed, whilst their leader perishes on the scaffold. *The Midnight Bell*, also stated to be a German story, and published in 1798, went through three editions, and was translated into French in 1799. It is the work of Francis Lathom, an eccentric actor and novelist. Said to be the illegitimate son of a distinguished peer, Lathom, who was wealthy, for a time seems to have been closely connected with the Norwich theatre. He retired, however, to a lonely farm in Aberdeenshire, where he died on May 19th, 1832. He has left some twenty novels and ten plays. *The Orphan of the Rhine*, which first appeared in four volumes, 1798, is by Mrs. Eleanor Sleath, of whom practically nothing is known save that she also wrote *Who's the Murderer? or, The Mysteries of the Forest*, 1802; *The Bristol Heiress*, 1808; *The Nocturnal Minstrel, or The Spirit of the Wood*, 1809; and *Pyrenean Banditti*, 1812. *Horrid Mysteries* we owe to the pen of Peter Will, sometime minister of the German Lutheran chapel in the Savoy. It is translated from the so-called *Memoirs of the Marquis of Grosse,* by a German author, Karl Grosse, who published several romances between 1790 and 1805, and who, to add a new zest to his melodramatic histories, dubbed himself "Marquis of Pharnusa." It was fiction such as this that Jane Austen was satirizing all too gently. A bolder corrective, however, was administered by Eaton Stannard Barrett, who in 1813 published his burlesque attack *The Heroine; or, The Adventures of Cherubina*, a piece of delicious fooling. Miss Cherry Wilkinson, half-crazed by reading nothing but the most sensational and blood-curdling fiction, disowns her father, an honest old yeoman of no small fortune, hight Gregory Wilkinson, and flies from his house. As she is leaving very secretly at dawn, in the greatest flurry, hurry, and distress, she deems it incumbent upon her there and then to compose a sonnet. At nightfall she enters a tumble-down barn. But no dead hand grasps hers and forcibly drags her in ; no flaming eyeball glares furiously through a crevice. It is really moſt disheartening ! Her further adventures in London and in a ruined caſtle when she tries to eſtablish herself with a retinue of servants are good fun. Eventually she is weaned from her follies, and Stuart, her lover, completes the cure with doses of *Don Quixote* and *The Vicar of Wakefield*.

The influence of Mrs. Radcliffe on her contemporaries can hardly be over-eſtimated. Every pen essayed to catch something of her ſtyle, to write of some peerless heroine persecuted by wicked marquis or villainous monk, imprisoned in a terrific caſtle or mouldering abbey, scared by apparitions and illusions caused by cracking doors, unaccountable noises, sudden gleams of light where no person could be walking, until at laſt Matilda, or Rosalia, or Imogene is rescued by her lover, and as the ſtory closes with this happy bridal it is discovered that the very caſtle or abbey where she had been secretly detained is part of her own domain now reſtored to her by the death of a cruel and treacherous relative. Smartly wrote Colman of the fiⅽtion that poured from the press—

> " A novel now is nothing more
> Than an old caſtle and a creaking door,
> A diſtant hovel,
> Clanking of chains—a gallery—a light—
> Old armour and a phantom all in white—
> And there's a novel ! "

Although it is quite impossible to give anything like a complete liſt of even the beſt known noveliſts who refleⅽt Mrs. Radcliffe's influence, a few names might be mentioned. One of the moſt notorious of the macabre romances is Matthew Gregory Lewis' *The Monk*,[1] which appeared in 1796. Not content with vaults and charnels, with the Wandering Jew and the Bleeding Nun, " Apollo's sexton," as Byron dubbed him, spiced his pages with schoolboy erotics, which caused considerable scandal, and led to a speedy suppression of the firſt edition. It was immediately reprinted in a slightly abridged form, but the fashion had been set, and writers such as Charlotte Dacre,

---

[1] *The Monk* was published at Paris (chez Maradan), 1797, in a translation by Deschamps, Desprès, Benoît, and Lamare, 4 vols., 12mo, and 3 vols., 12mo. There is another translation by Morellet, which appeared poſthumously in 1838. In 1840 appeared *Le Moine*, " trad. nouvelle et entièrement conforme au texte de la première édition anglaise, par Léon de Wailly," 2 vols., 18mo, Paris, Dellorge.

who assumed the name of Rosa Matilda, penned novel after novel with would-be piquant titles, *The Libertine, The Passions, The Confessions of the Nun of St. Omer*, which latter is dedicated to Lewis himself in admiring terms. All these and their kin are rather stilted, sometimes absurd, and as a matter of fact quite harmless.

In the preface to his first novel, *The Fatal Revenge* (1804), Charles Robert Maturin roundly declared that no source of emotion is so powerful or so universal as the " fear arising from objects of invisible terror," and his work is in truth drenched in horror, blackness, and gloom. His masterpiece, *Melmoth, the Wanderer*, published in 1820, is of excessive length and invention. The main theme is that of life prolonged by a mysterious compact, but narration is tangled with narration ; form and proportion are entirely lost. Nevertheless there are many passages of exquisite, if sombre, and unearthly beauty. Maturin's tragedies, in the best of which, *Bertram*, produced at Drury Lane, May 9th, 1816, Kean had a tremendous success, are one and all as wild and terrifying as his romances. In his dramatic work there can further be seen the influence of Schiller's *Die Raüber*, first made known to England in a paper read by Henry Mackenzie to the Royal Society of Edinburgh in 1788. The romanticism of Germany and its sentimentalism immediately coalesced with the romanticism of Mrs. Radcliffe and her followers and the sentimentalism both in fiction and on the stage of such authors as Cumberland, Holcroft, Mrs. Inchbald, and the younger George Colman. Monk Lewis, William Taylor, of Norwich, George Walker, Lathom, and Sir Walter Scott himself in his earliest work turned to German inspiration. This met with some terrible parody in *The Anti-Jacobin*, and there can be no doubt that Canning's *Rovers* had a much-needed and salutary effect. We must not forget the influence of Mrs. Radcliffe upon Scott, and more particularly perhaps upon Lord Byron.

The romances of William Godwin, especially *St. Leon*, with the hero's imprisonment in the dungeons at Constance, the escape from the Auto da Fé at Valladolid and his subsequent journey to the deserted mansions of his fathers, owe much to Mrs. Radcliffe. Shelley's chaotic tales *Zastrozzi* and *St. Irvyne* borrow some of their mad ideas from a distortion of Godwin's politics, the incidents being a mere nightmare phantasmagoria. Mary Shelley's shorter stories have merit, and *Frankenstein* is certainly not without considerable power, but the apocalyptic *Last Man*, which so deeply impressed Jefferson Hogg, and which Dr. Garnett commends, I confess I find almost unreadable. *The Vampire*, that rather ghastly little fragment of Byron's, from which Polidori, the young Italian doctor, made something of a story, is not to be forgotten. *The Canterbury Tales* of Sophia and Harriet Lee, twelve stories related by travellers thrown together by accident, are memorable for other reasons than that *Werner* is directly derived from the German's tale *Kruitzner*.

Rookwood, published in May, 1834, the best romance of William Harrison Ainsworth, whose talent, though very unequal, has been quite unduly depreciated of late, is confessedly founded on Mrs. Radcliffe. Says the author in his preface : " Wishing to describe somewhat minutely the trim gardens, the picturesque domains, the rook-haunted groves, the gloomy chambers and gloomier galleries of an ancient hall with which I was acquainted, I resolved to attempt a story in the bygone style of Mrs. Radcliffe (which had always inexpressible charms for me), substituting an old English squire, an old English manorial residence and an old English highwayman for the Italian marchese, the castle, and the brigand of the great mistress of Romance." Many of the novels of Bulwer Lytton, a far cleverer writer than nowadays is generally allowed, are of the same school. The works of Sheridan Le Fanu, whose *In a Glass Darkly* teems with imps, trances, spectres, are written with considerable skill and power. In 1848 Catherine Crowe issued *The Night Side of Nature*, which has been called " one of the best collections of supernatural stories in our language," a book which, it is to be feared, is almost forgotten to-day, but it has none the less many admirable pages and is assuredly deserving of a more lasting popularity. Lineal descendants are Dr. Frederick George Lee's *Sights and Shadows* (1894) and *More Glimpses of the World Unseen* (1878) and W. T. Stead's *Real Ghost Stories*.

Charles Brockden Brown, the first American novelist to count, is, especially in *Wieland ; or, The Transformation* (1798), steeped in the tradition of the macabre. *Arthur Mervyn* deals with the yellow fever which devastated Philadelphia ; *Edgar Huntley* tells the adventures of a sleep-walker, a somnambulist who commits a murder. Incidentally it may be noted that Brown's Red Indians are far less idealized than Fenimore Cooper's.

It is not necessary to do more than mention the name of Edgar Allan Poe.

At the same time as Ainsworth and Lytton, George William MacArthur Reynolds, Chartist and agitator, was penning his interminable and innumerable works. There is hardly one which is not of quite portentous length. All are replete with the most outrageous incidents and clap-trap melodrama, whilst history itself runs stark mad through his pages. *The Bronze Statue ; or, The Virgin's Kiss*, is a tale which centres round a gruesome instrument of torture similar to the Iron Maiden of Nuremburg ; *Pope Joan* relates the wild adventurings in Moorish Spain of that entirely mythical dame ; *The Parricide, Robert Macaire, The Necromancer* are titles which proclaim themselves. In *The Mysteries of London*, a huge romance, Reynolds details what Spaniards would call *la mala vida* of the metropolis in the first years of Victoria's reign, the gaming dens, St. Giles' Rookery, thieves' hotels, flash kens, body-snatching, burking, garrotting, and midnight ruffianism of every kind. It was Reynolds, too, who had the effrontery to write *Pickwick Abroad*, which was published in 1839, and had a sale of 12,000 copies. Again, bodily taking Hogarth's great pictures of " The Two 'Prentices," " The Rake's Progress," " The Harlot's Progress," and " Marriage à la Mode " to illustrate his chapters, he wove around them a tangle of lurid incidents which he called *Old London*. It is an easy transit from these *London Journal* romances to writers such as Proctor, George and William Emmett, Fox, J. F. Smith, the old-fashioned " penny-a-liner " Bohemians, who knocked about Fleet Street and produced " dreadfuls " and " shockers " galore. Degraded and incredibly vulgarized even here in the very dregs we can trace the influence of Mrs. Radcliffe, but put to what base use ! The gold is turned into vile dross ! There were also issued in the mid-decades of the nineteenth century novels, written by hacks and grub-street journalists, to which her name was unscrupulously affixed, or, at least, some name which must inevitably be mistaken for that of the author of *Udolpho*. Such is *Manfrone ; or, The One-handed Monk*, an utterly worthless compilation of ill-digested horrors and ranting absurdities, which in a late edition unblushingly bears on its title-page— " By Mrs. Radcliffe." It must be allowed that the first edition, 1809, is published as by Mary Anne Radcliffe, yet the work, with its vast gloomy apartments, melodramatic monks in sable cowls, heroines who peruse old chronicles of horrid import and swoon away, is a close imitation (more truly a parody) of *Udolpho* and *The Italian*.

Mrs. Radcliffe's romances, as we have seen, were translated into French immediately as they appeared. They passed swiftly from hand to hand, and in Paris became the rage. The circulating libraries could not provide copies enough : the booksellers reprinted them again and again.

In the Marquis de Sade's indiscreet satire on Josephine and the First Consul, *Zoloé*, published in Messidor VIII (July, 1800), the novels of the day are discussed by a fashionable assembly, and Volsange (Mde. Visconti) declaims against the prevalent anglomania. She " tears to shreds all that bombastic twaddle and those rank impossibilities which the authors of to-day delight to heap up in their novels, which they keep on endlessly repeating and accumulating. Those castles, those subterranean vaults and passages, those mysteries and tortures which have never existed save in the sickly imagination of the novelists themselves seemed to her nothing less than an outrage on common sense." Forbes, an English nobleman, undertakes the defence of English literature, and he is warmly supported by Zoloé (Josephine) and Lauréda (Mde. Tallien). This passage vividly shows us the literature which was chiefly in demand in French society a century and a quarter ago.

As fifty years later in mid-Victorian England, so then sundry novels appeared professing to be the genuine work of Mrs. Radcliffe, which are in reality only imitations of her more macabre incidents, hardly of her style. That they were popular is shown by *Les Visions du Château des Pyrénées*, a romance which ran into a second edition in 1810 and which purported to be translated from a novel of Mrs. Radcliffe's published at London seven years before. It is, in truth, an original tale by Count Garnier and Mdlle. Zimmermann. *Le Couvent de St. Catherine*, a romance of the thirteenth century, which was published in two volumes (1810), also feigned to be by the same pen that wrote *Udolpho*. It is an improbable story enough of the days of Edward I, unhistorical to a degree. In Italy romances occasionally appear even at the present day which bear Mrs. Radcliffe's name, but of which she is wholly innocent. Such a one is *Gli Assassini di Ercolano*, which was published at Milan in 1871, most profusely illustrated, " splendidamente illustrata ! " In justice, it must be

confessed that the French romances are as a rule of an infinitely
superior quality to the English false goods. The baron Léon
de la Motte-Langon, originally known as de la Motte-Houdan-
court, published two novels as translations from Mrs. Radcliffe
of which he was himself the sole author. The first, *L'Hermite
de la Tombe Mystérieuse*, professed to have been extracted by the
magician of *Udolpho* from some annals of the thirteenth century,
and to have been turned into French by de la Motte-Langon
(1815); the other, *Les Mystères de la Tour St. Jean*, also purported
to be a translation from Mrs. Radcliffe (1818).

Rose *d'Altenberg; ou, le Spectre dans les Ruines*, translated in 1830
by M. Henri Duval from an English MS. said to have been
found " in the portfolio of the late Ann Radcliffe," had already
appeared, seventeen years before, in 1813 as *Alexina*, a novel
in four volumes, imitated from the English by Madame Brayer
de Saint-Léon. Then Mrs. Campbell published a version of it
as her own work, London, 1821, under the title of *The Midnight
Wanderer*, so M. Duval only brought the *Wanderer* back to
native France when he re-translated it as *Rose d'Altenberg*,
recovered from the Radcliffe portfolio.

The more legitimate authors frankly allowed that their works
were " imité de l'Anglais d'Anne Radcliffe," an inscription
which frequently occurs on the title-page of novels by Madame
Ruault de la Haye. This lady was born about 1790, married
whilst quite a girl against the wishes of her family, and being
after a few years deserted by her husband, she was reduced
almost to want. She took to her pen for a livelihood, and writing
under the pseudonym of the Comtesse de Nardouet, became a
prolific purveyor of macabre romances. Hers is *Barbarinski ;
ou, les Brigands du Château de Wissegarde*, 2 vols. (1818), which
has a frontispiece illustrating a somewhat weird incident in the
story. Henri, the young, faithful, and brave valet of the hero,
Lord Wilson, having penetrated to the chapel of the dead, is
seen starting back from an open tomb whence rises a sudden
bright and sulphurous flame. In the frontispiece to *Le Panache
Rouge, ou le Spectre de Fer*, 2 vols. (1824), two damsels—the heroine
Ines and her confidante—are gazing through a grille into a
vaulted cell when they behold a carious skeleton chained to a
massy pillar. *Le Château de Sombremar, Le Chevalier aux Armes
Noires, Le Mystérieux Don Ténébros*, all partake of the same
quality, and the macabre and horrible are pushed to their utmost

limits. Yet withal Mde. de Nardouet has a certain knack of story-telling, and knows how to grip her readers' attention.

But greater names than this forgotten novelist owed allegiance to Mrs. Radcliffe. Honoré de Balzac thought her romances admirable, and many of his first efforts were directly inspired by her pages. In some of his maturer work their influence still prevails, as it often does in Dumas, Victor Hugo, Eugène Sue, Joseph Petrus Borel, Baudelaire—and when I have said Balzac and Baudelaire what more can I add ?

In English literature the macabre is not unrepresented to-day. We have the work of E. F. Benson, Bram Stoker, Algernon Blackwood, the Provost of King's, and many more. I am only too conscious that here and throughout this essay where I have mentioned one name I might have referred to a dozen, where I have cited one novel I might have numbered a score. So great has been the influence of the genius of Ann Radcliffe, a landmark, and a power in English literature. And that is praise enough.

JANE AUSTEN

JANE AUSTEN

IT has been said by a recent critic that when Jane Austen died on July 18th, 1817, "novels were not taken very seriously either by those who wrote or by those who read them. At least the novel was not recognized to be the predominant form of modern literature." The first part of this statement may not unfairly, I think, be said to be calculated to give a false and biassed impression; and, as regards the second pronouncement, even if it be candidly allowed that the novel was not then, perhaps, so entirely predominant as it was very soon to become and still remains to-day, yet great masters (notably Richardson), who took their work very earnestly, had already written, and fiction had certainly won thousands of avid readers who would seldom, if ever, turn to poetry and the essay, and when they did so it was from a sense of duty and polite improvement rather than from pleasure and inclination. "To read novels was to idle," continues the critic. But I venture to suggest that this was no more the case, and in intellectual circles no more considered to be the case, an hundred years ago than it is to-day. It is a dictum not infrequently heard now : and in which indeed we might well acquiesce did we confine ourselves to a casual glance at the fiction in highly-coloured and attractive wrappers that variegates the windows of smaller bookshops and stationers, or even to a more careful noting of the thin cheap novelettes which inevitably confront us in tubes and railway carriages at times when the crowds are thickest, early mornings and late afternoons ; but this, of course, is the froth and fritter hardly to be considered when we set to give sober judgement and appreciation. And as now, so a century ago, there were many whose narrow, rash, and trenchant opinion announced that novel reading was empty trifling, and a sheer waste of time. I am happy to believe that for twenty or thirty years past this puritan heresy has rapidly been losing ground and soon will be wholly extinct, but assuredly in the penultimate decade of the nineteenth century the circulating library was still suspect,

suspect as it was when Sir Anthony Absolute thundered out, " Madam, a circulating library in a town is as an evergreen tree of diabolical knowledge," and Mrs. Malaprop gave it as her opinion that they were " vile places indeed." Of course there still remain with us those—generally the very young—who rise superior to novel reading, and who exclaim, in Jane Austen's own words, " I am no novel reader. I seldom look into novels. Do not imagine that *I* often read novels. It is really very well for a novel." Most of us have heard the unthinking phrase, " Give me something light to read—a novel." " ' And what are you reading, Miss ——— ? ' ' Oh! it is only a novel! ' replies the young lady ; while she lays down her book with affected indifference, or momentary shame. ' It is only Cecilia, or Camilla, or Belinda ; ' or, in short, only some work in which the greatest powers of the mind are displayed, in which the most thorough knowledge of human nature, the happiest delineation of its varieties, the liveliest effusions of wit and humour, are conveyed to the world in the best-chosen language."

It would undoubtedly be a mistake to suppose that in Jane Austen's day fiction was not being taken seriously. Three years before her death John Colin Dunlop, a member of the Faculty of Advocates, had published in a set of octavo volumes " The History of Fiction ; being a critical account of the most celebrated prose works of Fiction, from the earliest Greek Romances to the Novels of the Present Day." A second edition was issued in 1816. In spite of numerous errors, few indeed when we consider the magnitude of his task, and for the most part such as can only be corrected by the recent results of scholarly research and more modern labours limited to particular periods and themes, in spite of many omissions—the literature of several northern countries, Germany, Scandinavia, Russia, is hardly mentioned—Dunlop's original work is in the main of permanent value, and, as far as his investigations extended, admirably documented and sound. His judgement and criticisms, if un-inspired, are almost always worth taking into account, whilst the detailed analyses of the many hundreds of romances noticed in his encyclopædic pages often prove in the highest degree useful and suggestive. I do not say that the specialist will find new light thrown upon his own pet corner, but I do assert that even to-day this " History of Fiction " taken as a whole is a most remarkable and significant achievement. In his fourteenth chapter, " Sketch of the Origin and Progress of the English Novel—Serious—Comic—Romantic," Dunlop, although he speaks at comparative length upon *Euphues*, Greene's *Philomela*, and Orrery's portentous *Parthenissa*, deals very briefly with subsequent fiction. Mrs. Behn is given a short and superficial paragraph, Mrs. Manley only a few words, Richardson, Fielding, and Smollett receive warm and understanding praise, but after touching upon some half-a-dozen writers, such as Walpole, Clara Reeve, Mrs. Frances Sheridan, and Godwin, the chapter concludes with a eulogy of Mrs. Radcliffe, a glance at some English *Voyages Imaginaires*, and an open acknowledgement that what has been treated altogether so inadequately might of itself have supplied matter for an equal number of volumes as comprise the complete study. The point is, not that English fiction was dealt with so disproportionately and with such arbitrary omissions, but that, especially as regards later and living writers, Godwin and Mrs. Radcliffe, it was seriously and studiously dealt with at all.

Jane Austen stands so pre-eminently above all her peers that some of us are a little apt to consider her as an isolated phenomenon almost without predecessors, without contemporaries of any note, with few and feeble imitators—rather a lonely figure in fiction. And so indeed she was—alone in her greatness of reserve and consummate power, but not alone historically, one of a long procession of female novelists, many of whom, albeit she immeasurably surpassed and overtopped them all, were women of culture, of brilliant talents, even of notable genius. And it is well perhaps to remember some of these, for by so doing we can in a degree gauge the exquisite rarity and perfection of Jane's accomplished work.

Our first woman novelist, Aphra Behn, has left us among her thirteen romances two at least, *Oroonoko* and *The Fair Jilt*, which must be acknowledged as masterpieces. Not inaptly described as " the first emancipation novel," *Oroonoko* originally appeared in the summer of 1688, and was being reprinted—the ninth edition—in 1759, in 1777, and as late as 1800. It is vivid, realistic, intensely dramatic, and had an enduring influence not only at home but on literatures other than English. Mrs. de la Rivière Manley, for whose *New Atlantis*, " full of Court and Party Scandal," Pope quizzingly prophesied immortality, had in her own day an immense and by no means undeserved reputation for wit and brilliancy. She was indeed a remarkable figure in the world of letters, and it has been truly said that " both Swift and Smollett were as novelists under real obligations to the *New Atlantis.*" Mrs. Mary Hearne, Mrs. Jane Barker, Mrs. Davys, Mrs. Sarah Butler, the sedate Mrs. Rowe, the moral Mrs. Penelope Aubin, who was so careful to inform her readers "I do not write for bread," all enjoyed considerable vogue and commanded a large following of admirers. A greater name than these is Eliza Haywood, the " Ouida of her day," as Sir Edmund Gosse cleverly dubs her, who in the six and thirty years of her activity produced over seventy works of various kinds, beginning with little amatory *novelle* of no value, but culminating in *The History of Miss Betsy Thoughtless*, " the first really domestic novel, according to modern ideas, that exists in the language," and the undoubted ancestry of *Evelina.*

In the mid decades of the eighteenth century, as, under the influence of the great masters, the novel became less and less the languishing erotic romance or fantastic picaresque miscellany, more and more the detailed study of character, of motive, of sentiment, and there resulted a deliberate concentration towards prose fiction, the lady novelists are legion indeed. In May, 1744, Sarah Fielding established herself in general favour with *David Simple*, a book of some mark ; in 1750, the omnipotent Dr. Johnson wreathed with laurels the brow of Mrs. Charlotte Lennox to celebrate the publication of *The Life of Harriot Stuart ;* in 1761, Mrs. Frances Sheridan, in her *Memoirs of Miss Sydney Bidulph*, with such success accumulated on the head of her innocent heroine every possible affliction that in the following year the book was translated both into French and German ; in 1777, the ultra-sentimental Mrs. Elizabeth Griffith issued her three-volume " Collection of Novels Selected and Revised " ; in the spring of 1788, Mrs. Charlotte Smith won profit and reputation with *Emmeline ; or, The Orphan of the Castle*, which is, in the candid judgement of Scott, " a tale of love and passion, happily conceived, and told in a most interesting manner." Ten years before this Miss Burney's *Evelina*, composed, it is said, in scraps and fragments whenever opportunity served, had attained a tremendous and deserved triumph. No story indeed since *Clarissa* had succeeded one half so well. Almost unreservedly applauded by Burke, crowned with the warmest approbation of the great dictator of letters, who roundly declared that there

were " passages which might do honour to Richardson," *Evelina,*
first published in January, 1778, ran into a fourth edition early
the following year. The world was not slow to applaud a new
faculty of accurate observation, a keen sense of humour and
characterization. Anecdotes began to multiply : the story went
that Sir Joshua Reynolds taking the book up whilst at table,
soon became so absorbed that he actually had to be fed whilst
reading it through. Now-a-days we recognize that *Evelina*
owes much of its charm to its spontaneity and the youthful
grace and freshness of its author. *Cecilia,* which followed in
1781, a confessedly ambitious and regularly written story of
love and family pride, is altogether heavier, dilatory, over-
deliberate, and slow. Amongst those whom for the most part
we may style, rather perhaps in form and feeling than strictly
in time, the more immediate contemporaries of Jane Austen—
leaving on one side the genius of Ann Radcliffe and her school
of romantic terror, together with the historical novels of Miss
Porter—the most notable names are Mrs. Inchbald, whose two
remarkable tales have seldom if ever met with the recognition
they deserve ; Maria Edgeworth, who commingled good and
bad, weakness and much excellence, prolix periods and sparkling
wit, with delightful Irish inconsequence ; Amelia Opie, whose
somewhat pallid work is chiefly interesting because of its connexion with the Godwin philosophy ; Lady Morgan, *The Wild
Irish Girl,* full of Celtic excitability by no means divorced from
the traditional eloquence and humour ; the veteran Hannah
More, by reason of her preternaturally dull *Coelebs in Search of a
Wife,* published in 1809 ; Susan Ferrier, the exquisite miniaturist
of smaller Scottish gentry, such as the Ladies of Glenfern and
Mrs. MacShake. Of all these writers not one but in her own
hour of fame eclipsed the modest reputation of Jane Austen.
Now-a-days few, if any, save the professed student of literature,
read *Nature and Art, Manœuvring, Adeline Mowbray, Florence
MacCarthy, Inheritance ;* even *Castle Rackrent* and *Patronage*
are best known to avowed enthusiasts of fiction. " When
I met Jane Austen," declared Sir Egerton Brydges, who
knew her personally, " I never suspected that she was an
authoress." As late as 1859, a writer in *Blackwood's Magazine*
spoke of her as " being still unfamiliar in men's mouths "
and " not even now a household word." To-day the world
is divided into the elect and the profane—those who admire

Jane Austen, and those (one shudders to speak the phrase)—who do not.

To us who recognize her supreme genius it is difficult to bear in mind that her writing was an altogether secondary matter; that the daily round of her simple commonplace life, the claims of the immediate family circle, of nephews and nieces, greedy for " long circumstantial " fairy tales from Aunt Jane; the minor events of small society; the little businesses and interests of middle-class country life; visiting; " the elegant stupidity of private parties "; evening games, " spillikins, speculation, and brag "; conversation; " the true art of correspondence "; " the dreadful epocha of mantua making "; housekeeping, " the torments of rice-pudding and apple dumplings "; all these absorbed her attention first. What is almost more astonishing to remember is that she composed her novels at a desk in the common sitting-room at Steventon parsonage or Chawton cottage, writing on small slips of paper which were quickly hidden away, or covered with a fair sheet when visitors came in, that none might suspect her occupation. There was, we are told, between " the front door and the offices [at Chawton] a swing door which creaked when it was opened, but she objected to have this little inconvenience remedied, because it gave her notice when anyone was coming." So she sat at her desk in the general parlour of the house, working quietly in the midst of continual domestic interruption, without impatience, without distraction, without complaint. When we consider the meticulous care with which every tiniest incident, every hint of character or expression, finds not only its inevitable place but logical consequence in the story, when we discern that each fact, each action, each thread is individually gathered up and not a stitch dropped, we realize that here is the impeccable perfection of consummate genius.

Incidentally it is interesting to note that with regard to Mrs. Behn, " we are told she could write a page of a novel or a scene of a play in a room full of people and yet hold her own in talk the while." Says Gildon : " She always writ with the greatest ease in the world, and that in the midst of company and discourse of other matters. I saw her myself write *Oroonoko*, and keep her own in discoursing with several then present in the room." But Aphra Behn is, it must be confessed, sometimes, though not often, just a little careless in the texture of her plays ; and her brilliant novels, of course, are much shorter than the three volumes of a century and a quarter after. She was writing hurriedly withal, literally writing for bread.

The whole fact is that for Jane Austen her characters lived ; they were real people. They did not merely pass into a page of a book and pass out. She knew them intimately. She knew their whims, tastes, reserves, weaknesses, prejudices, predilections, their very manner of speech, gait, dress. She was well acquainted with their past, she could foreshadow their future. She continued their histories, telling of events that occurred after the printed narrative had closed. So "Kitty Bennet was satisfactorily married to a clergyman near Pemberley, while Mary obtained nothing higher than one of her Uncle Philip's clerks, and was content to be a star in the society of Meryton." When Jane visited an exhibition in Spring Gardens in 1817, she wrote to Cassandra that she found there "a small portrait of Mrs. Bingley, excessively like her." "I went," continues the letter, "in hopes of seeing one of her sister, but there was no Mrs. Darcy. Perhaps, however, I may find her in the great exhibition. . . . Mrs. Bingley is exactly herself—size, shape, face, features, and sweetness ! There never was a greater likeness. She is dressed in a white gown with green ornaments, which convinces me of what I had always supposed—that green was a favourite colour with her. I dare say Mrs. D—— will be in yellow." On one occasion when speaking of *Emma* Jane Austen remarked that "Mr. Woodhouse survived his daughter's marriage, and kept her and Mr. Knightley from settling at Donwell about two years." She also disclosed that "the letters placed by Frank Churchill before Jane Fairfax, which she swept away unread, contained the word 'pardon.'" At another time she told her family that the "something rather considerable" which Mrs. Norris [in *Mansfield Park*] had given William Price upon his commission as Second Lieutenant of H.M. Sloop "Thrush" was exactly one pound.

When characters live in this way for their creators it is an unmistakable sign of the highest order of genius. So Balzac used to announce to intimates news from his world of fiction just as if he were speaking of real events. "Do you know who Félix de Vandenesse is going to marry ? " he once asked. "Why, a Mademoiselle de Grandville. The match is a first rate one. The Grandvilles are quite wealthy in spite of what Mademoiselle de Belleville has cost the family." Another story goes that when Jules Sandeau was telling Balzac news about a sick sister, the novelist suddenly interrupted him with " I am sorry—but now let us get back to the realities of life. Have you heard who is going to marry Eugénie Grandet ? " Even upon his death-bed when he knew there was no hope, and in answer to his eager question " How long have I to live ? " the doctor had replied, " You will hardly last the night," the silence was next broken by the sick man murmuring as to himself, " Ah, if I only had Bianchon [1] he would save me ! " Archibald Henderson, in his study of Ibsen, says, that when someone remarked to the great dramatist that Nora in *A Doll's House*, had an odd name Ibsen immediately replied, " Oh ! her full name was Leonora, but that was shortened to Nora when she was quite a little girl. Of course you know she was terribly spoiled by her parents." The people of his brain were often more real to him than actual human beings. " He knew the characters almost from birth, in ancestral hereditament, in the features of their environment, in nascent qualities of soul."

Considering the tremendous vogue of the novel in the early years of the last century, and how easily it would seem, in the majority of cases at any rate, literary celebrity, flamboyant if ephemeral, was to be attained, it is certainly altogether inexplicable that Jane Austen was not only not fêted and lionized by London society, but that throughout her whole lifetime she received practically no encouragement whatsoever and had not one literary correspondent. It is true that in 1811 her first published novel *Sense and Sensibility* appeared with the simple indication " By A Lady " on the title-page, and *Pride and Prejudice*, two years after, merely has " By the author of ' Sense and Sensibility.' " But although Jane did not exert herself to proclaim her authorship, neither was she anxious to conceal it, and her identity was at least well known before the publication of *Emma* in December, 1815, as whilst the three volumes were in the press Mr. Clarke, the librarian of Carlton House, intimated to her that His Royal Highness would graciously be pleased to accept the dedication of her new novel, and thus the book came out under royal patronage. This seems to have been the only public recognition she received. In itself the compliment was kindly and sincere, for the future George IV was a man of

[1] *Illusions Perdues : Splendeurs et Misères*, etc.

polished taste, and, it would appear, no half-hearted critic and appreciator. In the autumn of 1815 Jane had been nursing her brother Henry through a dangerous illness, and the physician who attended him happened also to be attached to the Prince. This doctor told her that not only was the Regent a great admirer of her novels, reading them often with keen enjoyment, but that he kept a set in every one of his residences. Mr. Clarke, the worthy librarian, a piece of stiff pomposity, soon evidenced his personal inability to understand and value the delicate and superfine genius of Jane Austen by impossible suggestions as to further novels, in one of which might be delineated " the habits of life, character, and enthusiasm of a clergyman, who should pass his time between the metropolis and the country, who should be something like Beattie's minstrel." Proceeding to make himself even more supremely ridiculous he advanced in crass earnest the amazing proposal that " an historical romance illustrative of the august House of Cobourg, would just now be very interesting." Jane's reply to this idle babble is a letter distinguished by the acutest self-judgement and soundest good sense. She writes : " You are very kind in your hints as to the sort of composition which might recommend me at present, and I am fully sensible that an historical romance, founded on the House of Cobourg, might be more to the purpose of profit or popularity than such pictures of domestic life in country villages as I deal in. But I could no more write a romance than an epic poem. I could not sit seriously down to write a serious romance under any other motive than to save my life ; and if it were indispensable for me to keep it up, and never relax into laughing at myself or at other people, I am sure I should be hung before I had finished the first chapter. I must keep to my own style and go on in my own way ; and though I may never succeed again in that, I am convinced that I should totally fail in any other."

It is apparent then that Jane Austen was sadly neglected by her contemporaries, and, indeed, it is only in recent years she has begun to come to her own. Enthusiastic admirers she has always had from the days when Scott· entered in his diary (March 14th, 1826), that oft-quoted passage, which in spite of its familiarity must by reason of its candour and truth be given yet once more : " Read again, and for the third time at least, Miss Austen's very finely written novel of *Pride and Prejudice*.

That young lady had a talent for describing the involvements, and feelings, and characters of ordinary life, which is to me the most wonderful I ever met with. The Big Bow-wow strain I can do myself like any now going ; but the exquisite touch, which renders ordinary commonplace things and characters interesting, from the truth of the description and the sentiment, is denied to me." The first complete edition of Jane Austen's works was published by Richard Bentley in 1833, sixteen years after her death, and there was no further collected edition until 1892. It sounds almost cynical to quote Samuel Rogers' pointed comment on the multitudinous progeny of the Minerva Press. " Now-a-days as soon as a novel has had its run, and is beginning to be forgotten, out comes an edition of it as a standard novel." The publication in 1870 of J. E. Austen Leigh's biography of his aunt, which included *The Watsons*, an unfinished but brilliant work, *Lady Susan* a character study in epistolary form, a cancelled chapter of *Persuasion*, and a fragment, seven weeks writing, to which the name *Sanditon* has been conveniently given, awoke considerable interest, which was to no small degree augmented by the *Letters* appearing in 1884 under the editorship of Lord Brabourne. In spite of being concerned, as their editor allows, with " the most ordinary details and most commonplace topics " the letters are only surpassed by the novels themselves, and it was a sad and fatal lapse from critical perception and nice judgement when a certain writer announced that in his opinion they were " trivial." Even to-day albeit editions of her works and studies of Jane Austen have multiplied apace she has not yet been granted by common consent that position which is all her own. Too often the critics, amongst whom are her appointed panegyrists themselves, prove timid, they venture and do not dare, they eulogize and are lukewarm, they speak of her faults and she had none. The fact is that the genius of Jane Austen is so impeccable, her writing so faultless, her touch so unwavering, her achievement so complete, that the very simplicity of perfection eludes and deceives those who are not, as it were, innately skilled to appraise the highest art in its most delicate and subtle refinements. We do not hesitate to assert that a full appreciation of the genius of Jane Austen is the nicest touchstone of literary taste.

Although Jane Austen was far too great an individual to be influenced by the current literature of her day she was nevertheless an omnivorous reader. As a critic she is eminently sane and perhaps a little severe, but she had the right to be so, and she is never niggard of praise. She especially delighted in fiction, and boldly avows her preference. In one place she writes, " As an inducement to subscribe [to her library] Mrs. Martin tells me that her collection is not to consist only of novels but of every kind of literature. She might have spared this pretension to our family, who are great novel readers and not ashamed of being so." In the preface to the first edition of *Northanger Abbey* (1818), written by her brother Henry, he tells us that her favourite poet was Cowper, her favourite author in prose Dr. Johnson. And yet what could be more essentially different from the crisp direct English of Jane Austen than the balanced periods and sonorous classicism of Johnson's elaborated rhetoric ? For all her admiration she never fell into the mistake of modelling her sentences on the equal swing of ornate phrase and mannered antithesis, a parlous error which led Fanny Burney, who in *Evelina* had been vivacious, energetic, and clear, to become in *Cecilia* so imitative of *The Rambler* that people whispered (foolishly perhaps) the great man must personally have supervised the work ; whilst in *Camilla* the only pages which are happy are those where she forgets her pattern and is content to be simply herself. Well might Walpole, with a sad shake of the head, say of Miss Burney, " Alas ! She has reversed experience ! " Jane Austen's praise of Miss Burney is very warm, her partisanship staunch, and she was, we know, in 1796 among the first subscribers to *Camilla*. It is worth noting that the name *Pride and Prejudice* was undoubtedly suggested by some sentences at the end of *Cecilia*. Jane's novel was originally called *First Impressions*, and under this title she often refers to it. But towards the close of *Cecilia* we read " The whole of this unfortunate affair has been the result of Pride and Prejudice," which last words are repeated twice on the same page each time in large type. There can be no question that hence Jane derived her alliterative title.

It is characteristic that the qualities in fiction which especially arouse Jane's dislike and incur her sharpest reprimands are any extravagance of language, affectation and unreal sentiment, improbabilities of plot or character, untidy incoherence of incident, and desultory disconnected adventures only introduced to startle and astound. Thus she wittily passes judgement on

Miss Owenson's [1] pseudo-Hellenic *Ida of Athens*. " It must be
very clever because it was written, the authoress says, in three
months. We have only read the preface yet, but her Irish girl
does not make me expect much. If the warmth of her language
could affect the body it might be worth reading this [January]
weather." Sir Samuel Egerton Brydges' *Fitz-Albini* [2] did not
please her. " There is very little story," she comments, " and
what there is is told in a strange, unconnected way. There
are many characters introduced apparently merely to be delineated."
Of *Clarentine*, a romance by Sarah Burney, the younger sister of
Madame D'Arblay, Jane says " We are surprised to find how
foolish it is. I remember liking it much less on a second reading
than at the first, and it does not bear a third at all. It is full of
unnatural conduct and forced difficulties, without striking merit
of any kind." *Self Control*, a novel which was published in
1810 [3] by Mary Brunton, the wife of a Scotch minister, justly
receives a like censure. " I am looking over ' Self Control '
again, and my opinion is confirmed of its being an excellently
meant, elegantly written work, without anything of nature or
probability in it. I declare I do not know whether Laura's
passage down the American river is not the most natural possible
everyday thing she ever does." These several criticisms (many
more of which on similar lines might be quoted) of long-for-
gotten novels seem to me of no little import and value as showing
us the standards by which she judged, the errors and extrava-
gancies she especially reproved. They afford us some insight
into the workings of her own mind, they give us her own
criterion, points of view of extreme significance when we
remember that no author was ever a more trenchant and deliberate
critic of self than was Jane Austen. We should particularly
notice that she never swerves from her honest unpretending
standard, that the books she disrelishes are condemned one and
all for the same sound reasons, and moreover, that she rarely
if ever blames until she had read the work more than once, that
her criticism is considered, careful, and slow.

The defects of most novelists of an hundred years ago, and
indeed of many novelists since, often arose from the fact that they

---

[1] Sydney Owenson (*ob.* 1859) married Sir Charles Morgan in 1812.
[2] *Arthur Fitz-Albini*, 2 vols., 1798. Second edition, 1799. This novel had
some popularity, but seems to us tame and artificial.
[3] It was reprinted as lately as 1852.

felt it an imperative duty to give their readers a tale of adventurous incident with a conventional ending to which character, psychology, and even sentiment were all subordinate. Mr. George Moore has an anecdote how Granville Barker once cycling in Ireland met at the foot of a hill a stranger. It was Furnivall, and, as they pushed their machines before them, they " discoursed literature." Barker " tarried over the mentality of his characters " and Furnivall cried out : " Get on with the story : it's the story that counts." This ancient dictum, a law they hardly dared to disobey, had for years been hanging like a millstone round the neck of the novelist, and in consequence as he drew towards the end of his work he almost inevitably found himself obliged to unravel an intrigue the ramifications of which, entirely superfluous in itself, he had either forgotten or was impotent to connect. And so we were perforce given chapters huddled to an unsatisfactory and mutilated conclusion, even more unconvincing than the wedding and conventional dance with a cue for the music which are wont to wind up the fifth act of a Restoration comedy. The faults of even our greatest writers often come from blind obedience to this discredited law, unfortunate source of how many redundant dull-brained chapters ! When we read *Oliver Twist* who cares about the exact relationship between Rose Fleming and Oliver, or the stereotyped and complicated confession of Edward Leeford *alias* Monks ? It is obvious, too, that Harry Maylie's anæmic love-affair and Rose's illness are the merest padding. With what relief we return to the matrimonial misfortunes of Mr. Bumble or the rascalities of the Artful Dodger ! It might well puzzle a reader who had even newly finished the last page of *Bleak House* to relate concisely the story of Nemo, Mr. George, and Mrs. Bagnet, or the Woodcourts, but Skimpole, Mrs. Jellyby, old Mr. Turveydrop, and Miss Flite could never be forgotten. It has been pertinently observed that in *Little Dorrit* at least Dickens does not seem clearly to have understood his own intrigue.[1]

At length, however, the novelists learned their lesson, and we realize to-day that fiction can have no artificial conventions nor trammelled restraints imposed upon it, and this for the simple reason that fundamentally it is the psychology that matters, that the author must " tarry over the mentality of his

---

[1] I am aware that this criticism has been stoutly controverted, but that it is fairly possible to make such a suggestion is very significant.

characters." This mentality, the sentiments, passions, ambitions, desires, he portrays will of themselves necessarily and logically give rise to all needful plot, circumstance, intrigue, and, it may be, even adventure. But such incidents, be they simple or complex, are primarily the correlative outcome of the expression and counterplay of the various emotions, energies, aims, instincts, and points of view, of his characters, not a stereotyped and extraneous frame-work of accident and coincidence into which at times he forces his figures to fit themselves, and, broadly speaking, those who are accommodated best are found to be the most bloodless, flaccid, and uninteresting : those who will not be coerced and arranged to order, virile, natural, and true. People are essentially more absorbing than melodramatic adventure and startling surprise. Emma Bovary proves more vital than Monte Cristo, the hectic and hysterical amours of an unknown village-doctor's wife a tale of greater interest and far more compelling power than the elaborate revenge-scheme of a mysterious multi-millionaire. In dogmatizing thus in somewhat general terms it may not be impertinent to guard against any seeming denial of the fascination of romance, but the craft of mere story-telling is explicitly on another and lower plane than the analysis of the emotions and the will.

If the novelist's characters live, however lowly their sphere, however limited their environment, they cannot fail to be interesting. And it is significant that the unity and continuity of many of our quite recent novels depend upon psychology, whilst plot is altogether subservient or even ignored. The novelist who puts his own mental experiences, his own knowledge into a work can dispense with the introduction of alien and unreal matter. Incident there must be perhaps, because character is so frequently determined and exhibited by incident, but this is often of the barest, most commonplace and everyday kind. And so in Mr. Compton Mackenzie's *Sinister Street*, particularly in the first part which is admittedly the best, in *Guy and Pauline*, and again in Mr. James Joyce's *A Portrait of the Artist as a Young Man*, it may fairly be said that plot does not exist, whilst if possible it is even more absent from Mr. Alec Waugh's *The Loom of Youth*, which is simply an extremely remarkable and deeply interesting account of the effect upon character of one of our smaller public schools, the home of method, punctuality, scheduled studies and systematized relaxations ; a formal atmosphere where beyond all others "shall each day just to his neighbour rhyme."

French writers, and of the first rank, recognized the essential importance of psychology more clearly than our English novelists. We only need to remember Huysmans and his famous work *A Rebours*, which is absolutely without action, being the study of a man whose habits, sympathies, and antipathies are presented in extraordinary detail. There are lengthy passages which describe precious stones, exotic perfumes, orchids, liqueurs, a picture by Gustave Moreau, the poems of Baudelaire. *En Route* has no more incidents than visits to various Paris churches and convents, and a ten days' retreat amid the utter silence and solitude of a Trappist monastery—la Trappe de Notre-Dame-d'Igny, near Fismes, la Marne. To take one example, too, from the many novels of the great master Zola—*Une Page d'Amour* is purely psychological, the only episodes being the illness of a little girl, a juvenile party, attendance at the parish church during the month of Mary (May), the child's death.

Mr. F. W. Cornish, in his study of Jane Austen (*English Men of Letters*), notices not without sound acumen that Louisa Musgrove's accident on the Cobb at Lyme is the only incident in *Persuasion*—"one may almost say the only incident in all the novels." It is indeed the only incident on which attention is concentrated, the only incident that interrupts and changes to some extent the course of the action, giving rise to a new series of not altogether expected results. By their very titles, *Pride and Prejudice* and *Sense and Sensibility*, show that the motif of these tales is concerned with the consequences of a diversity of judgement and mental outlook, with emotions and sentiments. There is an interesting comment on this in a letter to Cassandra, when, having visited the "Liverpool Museum" and the "British Gallery," Jane writes : "I had some amusement at each, though my preference for men and women always inclines me to attend more to the company than the sight."

In the whole of English literature there are no such men and women as Jane Austen's, the only figures which do not suffer by comparison with hers being the men and women of Shakespeare himself. She has given us a very large number of characters, some lightly sketched, some drawn at full length, but every one, although many possess the same traits, the same foibles, the same mannerisms, is as perfectly discriminated and

as completely individual as though each were endued with the
most peculiar, unique, and totally distinct qualities. Mrs.
Bennet, Mrs. Jennings, Mrs. Allen, three matrons, are confirmed gossips, rather empty-headed if good-natured and warm-
hearted, busy with trifles, comfortable, full of trivial talk and
empty ejaculations, bustling, complacent, without one distinguishing feature, and yet each is absolutely individual although
each has so much in common with the others.   Lady Catherine
de Bourgh and Mrs. Norris are both domestic tyrants, insolent
to their inferiors, intensely disagreeable, bitter, ill-tempered,
harsh, selfish and overbearing, but they are two quite separate
personalities, each with manners, speech, expression proper to
herself alone.   Aunt Norris, indeed, is one of Jane Austen's
most wonderful figures, a character so perfectly drawn as, in
her own line, never to be equalled, far less excelled in any
literature I know.   In her recent admirable work on Jane
Austen, Signora Emilia Bassi is of much the same opinion :
" Mansfield would not be Mansfield without her," she cries,
and she thinks " *Mansfield Park* the most delightful of all " the
novels.   Here she is in full accord with Tennyson, and with
the group of famous men met by Goldwin Smith at a country
house who, when asked to name their favourite novel, " voted
unanimously " for *Mansfield*.   Yet we can hardly allow that
Mrs. Norris is better than Miss Bates, the scatter-brained,
inconsequent, eternally garrulous, tiresome, benevolent old
chatterbox, whose vapid talk flows on and on without pause,
let, or stay.

    The power to describe, and so perfectly describe, the common-
place characters of ordinary, everyday life, must be recognized
as one of the most salient features of Jane Austen's genius.   It
was chiefly for this that Lord Macaulay named her next after
Shakespeare, and Archbishop Whateley has the shrewd sentence,
" It is no fool that can describe fools well."   It is notable that
when some of her figures are a little eccentric, there is never any
insistence upon their whimsicality.   We realize that it exists
and no more ;   there is never the least over-emphatic note, no
high-colouring which too often becomes caricature, none of
that repetition which too easily becomes burlesque.   Exaggera-
tion is a facile but fatal fault, fatal in that the more it is indulged
the further we get from nature.   And so among the characters
of Dickens, much as we delight in them, we feel that sometimes

they tend to become comicalities rather than realities ; some catchword, some tag, highly effective if sparingly spoken, is used once too often, some distinguishing feature is unduly insisted upon in season and out of season. Thus the drowsiness of the Fat-Boy ; the glossy whiskers and " oh demmit ! " of Mr. Mantalini ; " ain't I volatile ? " ; the gleaming teeth of Mr. Carker ; the 'umility of Uriah Heep, are worn rather thin and bare with constant reiteration. We feel that there is something retrograde, a distinct throw back in the direction of the " humour," which became almost mechanical even in the hands of the great master, Ben Jonson, when not at his highest and best. We are gravitating towards types rather than individuals. Already labels are given such as Lord Frederick Verisopht, the foolish young nobleman ; Sir Mulberry Hawk, the preying sharper ; Mr. Pluck and Mr. Pyke, the humbler parasites. Soon we shall have Lord Lovechase " a Lover of Foxhunting and Country Sports " ; Lord Brainless, " a Pert, Noisy, Impertinent Boy " ; Mr. Snarl, " an old pettish Fellow " ; Mrs. Termagant, " a furious, malicious, revengeful Woman," as in the comedies of D'Urfey and Shadwell.

Jane Austen's fine art would not, of course, for a moment have admitted of such obvious ticketing. She seldom even introduces her characters with any preliminary description. They reveal themselves naturally as they talk, as we listen to them. What could throw more light upon Mr. Woodhouse's valetudinarian habits and gentle listless ways than his ruminations as he criticizes the portrait of Harriet Smith, who is depicted seated in a garden on a summer day ? " It is very pretty," he murmurs, " so prettily done ! Just as your drawings always are, my dear. I do not know anybody who draws so well as you do. The only thing I do not thoroughly like is that she seems to be sitting out of doors, with only a little shawl over her shoulders ; and it makes one think she must catch cold." " But, my dear papa," Emma explains, " it is supposed to be summer ; a warm day in summer. Look at the tree." " But it is never safe to sit out of doors, my dear," answers the father. How could Mrs. Palmer's silliness be more effectually shown than by her well-meaning philippic against Willoughby when she hears of his desertion of Marianne ? " She was determined to drop his acquaintance immediately, and she was very thankful she had never been acquainted with him at all. She wished

with all her heart Combe Magna was not so near Cleveland ;
but it did not signify, for it was a great deal too far off to visit ;
she hated him so much that she was resolved never to mention
his name again, and she should tell everybody she saw, how
good-for-nothing he was." A page of analysis could not better
display the self-satisfied conceit of the fatuous John Thorpe than
his reply when Catherine expresses a fear that her brother's gig
may break down. " Break down ! " he bawls, " Oh, Lord !
Did you ever see such a little tittuppy thing in your life ? There
is not a sound piece of iron about it. The wheels have been
fairly worn out these ten years at least—and as for the body !
Upon my soul, you might shake it to pieces yourself with a touch.
It is the most devilish little rickety business I ever beheld !
Thank God ! we have got a better. I would not be bound to
go two miles in it for fifty thousand pounds." And upon
Catherine, in a scare, entreating him to turn back and warn her
brother how unsafe it is he rattles on : " Unsafe ! Oh, Lord !
What is there in that ? They will only get a roll if it does break
down ; and there is plenty of dirt, it will be excellent falling.
Oh, curse it ! the carriage is safe enough if a man knows how
to drive it ; a thing of that sort in good hands will last above
twenty years after it is fairly worn out. Lord bless you ! I
would undertake for five pounds to drive it to York and back
again without losing a nail."

It is probably her consummate genius for the subtle exposition
of character in this spirited and natural way, the delicate finesse,
wit, and ease of her conversations, which have led several critics
of no mean rank to compare Jane Austen to comedy and the great
comic dramatists. The thought is an excellent and penetrating
one, but the comparison must be determined. A nice dis-
crimination is needed here. We cannot sweepingly compare
the Austen novels to the " Comedy of Manners " so called, for
the simple reason that this last phrase has owing to its misuse
become so vague, ambiguous, and distorted that before employing
it we are bound to define our terms. Many of the less accurate
and understanding critics, who are ingenuously careful to avoid
so doing, albeit the phrase is ever on their tongues, would
appear to limit " Comedy of Manners " to the Orange theatre—
I use that excellent nomenclature of Sir Edmund Gosse—with
perhaps Etherege's best play, a piece or two of Wycherley's and
a couple by Sheridan. They do not see that *Bartholomew Fair*,

and *A Chaste Maid in Cheapside* are full as striking examples of
the " Comedy of Manners " as *The Way of the World* or *The
Plain-Dealer*. To compare anything of Jane Austen's to *Bartholomew Fair* would be manifestly absurd, but between her novels
the *The Way of the World* there is a close resemblance of its
kind—they are of the same stock. We can then compare Jane
Austen's pages to the scenes of conversational comedy, of which
The Way of the World is so complete a specimen that the action
is almost static, the plot nugatory to the essence of the play.
Now a conversational comedy generally belongs to the " Comedy
of Manners," but the reverse emphatically need not hold true.
With regard to *The Way of the World* in his classic work on
Congreve Sir Edmund Gosse pertinently writes : " Many parts
are not to be turned over, but to be re-read until the psychological subtlety of the sentiment, the perfume of the delicately
chosen phrases, the music of the sentences, have produced their
full effect upon the nerves. But, meanwhile, what of the action ?
The reader dies of a rose in aromatic pain, but the spectator
fidgets in his stall, and wishes that the actors and actresses would
be doing something. . . . We have slow, elaborate dialogue,
spread out like some beautiful endless tapestry, and no action
whatever." It would really need an elegantly accomplished
connoisseur of literature to appreciate the full flavour of these
scenes at a first hearing, and in the theatre of Dutch William
elegantly accomplished connoisseurs of literature, if perhaps not
quite so scarce as now, did not at any rate comprise the bulk
of the audience. Dryden, with his unerring critical genius, had
hit the mark in his pregnant lines on Southerne's *The Wives'
Excuse ; or, Cuckolds Make Themselves*, a brilliantly conversational
but completely static comedy which, produced at Drury Lane
eight years before Congreve's masterpiece, had been something
very like a failure. The great poet has a couplet in the address
to his friend :

> " The Hearers may for want of *Nokes*[1] repine,
> But rest secure, the Readers will be thine."

Pit and gallery demanded the favourite low comedian and
his broad pranks, they were not able to listen to scene after scene
of exquisitely cadenced prose without drollery or even action.
In the library there is leisure to read and re-read, to ponder, to

---

[1] James Nokes, *ob*. December, 1692, the leading low comedian of the day.

digest and assimilate; in the theatre only the most cultivated faculty and attuned ear can readily appreciate and delight. It requires an education to enjoy upon the stage *Le Misanthrope* or *The Way of the World*. And this is because they are of the very refined quintessence of comedy, and it is to these that I would compare the novels of Jane Austen.

Every reader must have remarked that although the novels so faithfully and in such detail represent men and manners of an hundred years ago, a century of enormous and unprecedented changes, revolutions in thoughts, ideas, customs, constitutions, knowledge, social standards, in each branch and part of life, fresh and entirely natural do they remain even to-day. The scenes of Miss Burney or Miss Edgeworth with all their vigour and charm often seem quaint, old-fashioned, and singular; but not one mote of dust, not one fleck through all the long years has settled on the pages of Jane Austen. We may notice here a not impertinent point which has often been brought out, and which seems particularly to have struck Signora Emilia Bassi in her study *La Vita e le Opere di Jane Austen e George Eliot*. Although Jane Austen lived and wrote at an hour when Europe, as now, was convulsed in the throes of colossal war and great happenings that thrilled the world, yet throughout her books and her letters we find no hint, nor echo of these stupendous occurrences, no mention of Trafalgar and Waterloo. The freshness of Jane Austen's novels has been especially noted by Mr. Austin Dobson, who says: "Going over her pages, pencil in hand, the antiquarian annotator is struck by their excessive modernity, and after a prolonged examination discovers, in this century-old record, nothing more fitted for the exercise of his ingenuity than such an obsolete game at cards as 'casino' or 'quadrille.'" Nor is there reason for puzzle or surprise in this: it is indeed of the essence of her genius that the merely accidental finds so small a place in her writings. This, too, is the essence and the greatness of the genius of Shakespeare, of Molière, of Chaucer, of Cervantes. They dealt not with types but with humanity, with living men and women who cannot change however the world may alter and disguise itself about them. It is only the highest genius that can thus inevitably concentrate upon what is vitally and eternally true, disregarding the ephemeral and adventitious however large and important they may be waxing for the moment.

In this infallibly sure discardment of the non-essential and the extraordinary perfection that so logically results we may compare the flawless pages of Jane Austen with the work of Flaubert, and that which with the greatest of French novelists was a titanic process and an evocation of toil and agony with Jane Austen also is shown to have been no easy and spontaneous matter, for, although she was evidently from the first an exceptionally careful and deliberate writer, we know that she kept on revising and polishing with assiduous and loving care. She herself speaks of " the little bit (two inches wide) of ivory on which I work with so fine a brush as produces little effect after so much labour." Both attain the same result—a certain impeccability. A character is summed up and absolutely summed up in one sentence, and we feel that is the only one sentence which could so completely and definitely portray that character. Many authors have hoped to·accomplish this consummate finish by the accumulation of a copious mass of detail. Nothing is too small or too trivial to escape their observation and be particularized in their chapters. We admire their industry, we envy their energy, we covet their omnipercipience, but never once, in spite of much splendid work and unflagging perseverance, can they arrive at the result which alone is all-sufficient, which is given us so inevitably by the genius of a Flaubert or a Jane Austen.

On the morning of July 18th, 1817, Jane Austen passed away at the early age of forty-one, leaving only six fully completed books, but each one of these is quite perfect. Her life had been simple and placid, led for the most part amongst country surroundings, full of quiet joys, but not without domestic sorrows. And yet with all her limited experience she has produced work of so exquisite a rarity that if sheer perfection be the standard we must place her first of all English novelists. And when we remember the great names of Richardson and Fielding, of Dickens and Thackeray, of Meredith, James, and Hardy, we realize what praise and honour this conveys. Yet I cannot think it excessive. For in the pages of Jane Austen nowhere do we find a dull superfluity, nowhere do we find a failure, nowhere do we find a passage which might conceivably have been better said, nowhere do we find a fault. Indeed, I would with reference to her, echo the question which the sophist once put to Menander, and say " Jane Austen, Jane Austen and life, which of you two has copied the other ? "

BYRON'S "LOVELY ROSA"

BYRON'S "LOVELY ROSA"

Far be't from me unkindly to upbraid
The lovely ROSA's prose in masquerade,
Whose strains, the faithful echoes of her mind,
Leave wondering comprehension far behind.

English Bards and Scotch Reviewers, 1809, ll. 519–522.

THE orthodox note on the above passage runs thus: "The lovely little Jessica, the daughter of the noted Jew K——, seems to be a follower of the Della Crusca School, and has published two volumes of very respectable absurdities in rhyme, as times go; besides sundry novels in the style of the first edition of the Monk." Coleridge, in his edition of Byron (I., p. 357), gives us an additional sentence: "She has since married the *Morning Post*—an exceeding good match; and is now dead—which is better. B. 1816." We are further told that the last seven words are in pencil, and, possibly, by another hand.

King was a noted money-lender of the day, who is said to have dealt almost exclusively with the peerage. He seems to have been a man of address and talent in his line, and even to have had pretensions to taste and patronage as regards the fine arts. Especially was he famous for his excellent dinners, much frequented by the wits, when sometimes the highest personages of the realm were not strangers to his table. Sheridan was often his guest at his villa on the Thames, a palatial residence, fitted up by Walsh Porter in the Oriental style. His town house was in Clarges Street, and particularly remarkable shone his gorgeous equipage, which "advertised his calling." "A yellow carriage, with panels emblazoned with a well-executed shield and armorial bearings, and drawn by two richly-caparisoned steeds, the jehu on the box wearing, according to the fashion of those days, a coat of many capes, a powdered wig, and gloves *à l'Henri Quatre*, and two spruce footmen in striking but not gaudy livery with long canes in their hands, daily made its appearance in the Park from four to seven in the height of the season." Mrs. King, a fine woman, dressed in the latest mode, was usually to be seen in this chariot. Gronow, whose description is the above, records a mot uttered by Brummell when Lord William L——, on being thrown from his horse, was placed in the yellow carriage and conducted home by the obliging Mrs. King. "Aha," quoth the beau, " here we have a Bill *Jewly* (duly) taken up and honoured."

There is no mention however to be found of King's daughter, and Coleridge justly questions if in Byron's lines there is not some confusion between this young lady and " Rosa Matilda," [1] Charlotte Dacre, who married William Pitt Byrne, Robinson's successor as editor of the *Morning Post*, and who wrote under this Della Cruscan pseudonym. Charlotte Dacre, who is unnoticed in the *Dictionary of National Biography*, was born in 1782. She must have died before April 28th, 1842, since on that date Byrne married Julia Busk, the second daughter and fourth child of Hans Busk, scholar and poet. Julia Byrne was also an authoress who wrote several volumes of travel and foreign studies. She died as late as March 29th, 1894, at her residence, 16, Montagu Street, Portman Square, her husband having predeceased her by more than thirty years, April 8th, 1861. Charlotte Dacre published the following works : *Hours of Solitude*, poems, 2 vols. 8vo, Hughes, June, 1805, 14*s.* ; *Confessions of the Nun of St. Omer*, a romance, 3 vols., Hughes, 1805, 13*s.* 6*d.* ; *Zofloya, or The Moor*, a romance, 3 vols., Longman, June, 1806, 13*s.* 6*d.* ; *The Libertine :* a novel by " Charlotte Dacre, better known as Rosa Matilda," 4 vols., Cadell, April, 1807 ; *The Passions*, a novel " by Rosa Matilda," 4 vols., Cadell, June, 1811, 21*s.* ; *George the Fourth*, " A Poem . . . to which are added Lyrics designed for various Melodies," 1 vol., Hatchard, 1822.

Hours of Solitude, effusions " part the production of my untaught youth, and part of my later years," supplies as frontispiece a portrait of Rosa Matilda. She appears an elegant dark-haired, liquid-eyed damsel, who might well be of Hebraic parentage. The bare random titles of the poems will give some idea of the two volumes : *Passion Uninspired by Sentiment ; To Lindorf ;*

---

[1] It must be remembered that Anna Matilda, who was scarified by Gifford, is Mrs. Hannah Cowley, the skilful dramatist and poetess (1743–1809).

The Musing Maniac (written at eighteen) ; *The Murderer*, which in fine frenzy commences thus :

> Silent he ſtalk'd, and ever and anon
> He shudder'd and turn'd back, saying " Who follows ? "
> Horror had blanch'd his cheek ; his writhing brows
> Confess'd the inward ſtruggles of his mind.
> E'en in the diſtant, ever-varying clouds
> His tortur'd fancy form'd a vengeful angel,
> Pointing the sword of juſtice o'er his head,
> And e'en the murm'ring zephyrs, rushing by,
> Seem'd the low whisp'ring of the reſtless shade
> His sanguinary ſteel had forc'd abroad.

That's good ; " forc'd abroad " is good.   Other pieces are *Fog, Mildew, Froſt, Thaw, The Evil Being, L'Absence, Lasso a Me !, Madness, To Sympathy*, which begins :

> Sweet Sympathy ! Thou fair, celeſtial maid,
>   Thou precious, soft, indefinable tie,
>   Source of the pitying drop that dims the eye,
> Source of the sigh to Friendship's sorrows paid.

We also have *The Mountain Violet* (written at seventeen); *Experience* (written at eighteen—a charming paradox); *Tu es Beau comme le Desert, avec toutes ses Fleurs et toutes ses Brises :*

> Oh ! my soul's lord ! to my enamour'd eye
>   A fairer person lives not ; turn not then
> In soft confusion from me—nor deny
>   Mine eyes to gaze on thee alone of men.

Which let us hope apoſtrophizes Mr. Byrne, although I am afraid it does not.
" The Miſtress " thus addresses " the Spirit of her Lover." " Can I not press thee to my bosom ? Oh ! miserable mockery ! thou would'ſt evaporate in my embrace."   There are also verses written under the romantic signature of Azor, a favourite name with Rosa Matilda :

When I swore that I lov'd you, and lov'd you to madness,
    My words they were broken, my eyes overflow'd ;
When you own'd that *you* lov'd, my heart bounded with gladness
    I felt of my bliss as the bliss of a god.

And *A l'Oreiller de ma Maitresse :*

> Sweet pillow ! on whose down the loveliest fair
>   That e'er in slumber clos'd her radiant eyes,
> Reclines, her wasted spirits to repair,
>   That hence recruited, lovelier she may rise.

Weymouth is sentimental ; *Julia's Murder*, horrid ; *The Skeleton Priest, or The Marriage of Death*, a title which would have entranced Beddoes, highly reminiscent of *Alonzo and the Fair Imogene ; A Song of Melancholy* almost Ossianic with its " Dark as the wintry midnight is my soul ; sad and tempestuous. Fain would I sit upon the stern brow'd rock, listening to the roaring of the terrible cataract," which seems an echo of Beattie's Edwin. I suppose that minor, very minor, poetry of all ages merely differs in form, and the impressionistic Cartwheels or Parallelopipeds which (I believe) prevail to-day are infinitely more absurd than were the contents of Miss Simpkinson's album.

George the Fourth, " A Poem : Dedicated to the Right Honourable the Marquis of Londonderry," cannot be taken very seriously. Yet it opens heroically enough :

> Expanding far o'er Albion's wide domains,
> Where never-vanquish'd, heaven-born Freedom reigns,
> Prolific Commerce sheds its genial rays,
> While grateful myriads hymn their monarch's praise,

notwithstanding Greville thought that the Court presented " every base, low, and unmanly propensity, with selfishness, avarice and life of petty intrigue and mystery." Nevertheless the King is hailed as

> Patron of Genius !   Faith's unshaken friend,

and there is really humour when he is bidden

> Think thy great Sire from realms of brightest day
> Beholds well pleased—directs thy destin'd way.

The seventeen lyrics and four little odd pieces which go to make up this slim duodecimo are sugary enough, *The Mountain Cot*, for example, commences thus :

> How happy is the woodman's life !
>   Contented with his lowly lot,
> Ere the lark sings his matin lay,
>   He leaves his humble mountain cot.

It is really surprising how a writer who revelled in such vapid lyricism can have written romances which, however imitative and sensational, are undeniably interesting, and of their kind admirably contrived and related.

The Confessions of the Nun of St. Omer is dedicated in admiring terms to Matthew Gregory Lewis. This romance deals with the adventures of Cazire, daughter to the Marquis Arieni. At the opening of volume one the Marquis, having ruined himself by extravagance and loose living, flies to Italy with little Cazire, his favourite child, who is aged eight, leaving his deserted wife to retire to a romantic cottage. On his journey, in fact at the very first " locanda " where he halts, Arieni meets a beautiful countess, usually termed " the Rosendorf," with whom he soon forms a permanent but no very honourable connexion. A little later Cazire is introduced to Louis St. Elmer, and precociously falls in love with him. She is, however, incontinently consigned to the Convent of St. Omer to be educated by the nuns. Here she indulges in a course of " Dangerous Reading," and is furnished " clandestinely with volumes as romantic as the most avaricious fancy could desire." After several years spent in these delights she leaves the convent, and again encounters St. Elmer. Expressing himself shocked at her ultra-Gothic and impetuous views of life and conduct, he suddenly withdraws himself from her society and departs nobody knows whither. Cazire bemoans his loss for a time, but is consoled by the attentions of Augustus Fribourg, a necessitarian, who talks a vague philosophy through several chapters and makes ardent love to her meanwhile. She soon yields, in spite of the fact he is a married man, and in spite of the warnings of Ariel, a mysterious correspondent, who keeps conveying letters to her in some occult manner. Cazire next engages in a liaison with " a son of pleasure," Lindorf, whose person " was more than elegant. It was too beautiful for man ! " Disregarding an urgent missive from Ariel, who assures her that Lindorf is married, she flies with this Adonis to his home, where she makes the acquaintance of his sister Olivia and a friend. One morning the friend and the paragon are missing, whereupon the wretched Cazire is informed by Olivia that she is in reality no relation to Lindorf, but has merely been the mistress of the friend. Count Loretti, a very equivocal personage, next appears on the scene, but Cazire, weary of intrigue, seeks refuge at the house of a poor widow, whose daughter, Janetta, becomes her devoted attendant. Olivia presently offers her money which she rejects with fine scorn, and heroically taking from a drawer " various compositions, the produce of leisure hours," she submits these to a bookseller, who *more suo* informs her she will get " fame without emolument!" She is now arrested for a debt of twenty sequins at the suit of the Lady Olivia di Orno, and being penniless, is hurried off to jail. In prison a boy, Lindorf's child, is born. After a day or two, however, a sumptuous carriage sent by Ariel conveys her to a magnificent palace, and that evening the mystic Ariel himself appears in the person of St. Elmer, " the real lover." Cazire weds St. Elmer, but alas! finds she cannot love him. Very humanly she remarks " Had you but one error it should be dearer to my heart than all your virtues." One night a man, wounded in a street brawl, takes refuge in their house. It is Fribourg. Anon his old passion blazes out again, when Cazire " seals destruction in his arms." Immediately she is struck with remorse and attempts suicide, but the pistol misses, and she " falls en-horrored [1] to the floor." Presently St. Elmer, discovering his wife's guilt, challenges Fribourg, only to be brought home dying from the field of honour. Fribourg, pursued by the officers of justice, shoots himself, while the wretched Cazire, consigning her child to the care of her mother, and presenting Janetta with her "palazzo," retires to St. Omer's to take the veil, and presumably to write her memoirs. The incidents and adventures are, as may be seen, both melodramatic and intricate, but in spite of crudities and even absurdities not a few, there are striking, forceful passages in *The Confessions of the Nun of St. Omer*, and not infrequently we meet with speeches and situations that of their kind prove effective enough.

Zofloya, or The Moor, which appeared in June, 1806, an even more sensational and extravagant melodrama than Charlotte Dacre's first romance, is throughout accusingly imitative of Lewis' The Monk. It had none the less an extraordinary vogue at the time, and in 1812 there was published at Paris, four volumes, chez Barba, *Zofloya, ou Le Maure, histoire du XVe Siècle*, " traduite de l'Anglais par Mme. de Viterne." Mme. de Viterne was also responsible for French versions of The Nun of Misericordia (1807), an entirely typical novel by the prolific Sophia L.

1 " Enhorrored " is not to be found in the *New English Dictionary*.

Francis, and of Francis Lathom's *The Unknown, or The Northern Gallery* (1808). Victoria de Loredani, the central figure of *Zofloya*, is proud, passionate, and cruel, but lovely beyond compare, qualities which are incidentally shared by her brother Leonardo. All the wealth and beauty of Venice grace her birthday fête, when there appears on the scene Count Adolphus, bearing a letter of introduction to the Marquis de Loredani. Adolphus, a gallant who would have been termed in Restoration days "a general undertaker," *i.e.*, a promiscuous libertine, repays the hospitality afforded him by abducting Laurina, the Marquis' wife, who is still a woman of infinite charm. Victoria is left to be the sole comfort of her dishonoured father. For some not very obvious reason Adolphus after a long interval returns, and in a duel kills the Marquis. Laurina now persuades Victoria to fly with her and Adolphus to Montebello. Here the Count of Berenza falls in love with Victoria, but as this does not suit the plans of Adolphus the guilty pair take Victoria on a visit to la Signora de Modena, a sour old beldame, who conveniently dwells in the midst of an almost inaccessible forest. Victoria, deserted by her mother and the count, soon finds herself a close prisoner in the signora's charge. None the less she escapes after a while, and makes her way to Venice, where she again meets Berenza, who lodges her in a mysterious palace. Berenza tells her that he has been loved by a fair courtezan named Megalina Strozzi, whose advances he rejected. One night Victoria discovers a masked man about to poniard the sleeping Berenza. As the intending assassin escapes his face is unveiled and it proves to be Leonardo. Having fled from home after his mother's abduction, he has met with many adventures and finally become the accepted lover of Megalina, at whose instigation he seeks to murder Berenza. Terrified at the failure, this worthy couple incontinently leave Venice and seek a refuge in Capri. Berenza marries Victoria, but five years after their solemn nuptials there arrives at the palace Henriquez, his brother, of whom Victoria promptly becomes enamoured. Henriquez, however, is about to wed Lilla, a maiden of transcendent loveliness. Zofloya, the Moor, Henriquez's servant, is a paragon of every accomplishment, and a universal favourite. This excites the jealousy of a fellow-servant, Latoni, who stabs the Moor, and casts the body into the canal. A few days after, Latoni, seized with a sudden illness, confesses his crime, and, almost as he speaks, expires. A little later Zofloya returns to the palace to relate how he was picked up by a fisherman, who tended his wounds and nursed him back to health. An indefinable attraction now begins to draw Victoria to Zofloya, and she does not hesitate frequently to meet him at sunset in retired and lonely spots. She makes him her confidant, candidly avowing her love for Henriquez. The Moor supplies her with poison with which she experiments on her husband. Lest suspicion should be aroused, as his health fails, she accompanies him to Torre-Alto, his remote castle in the Apennines, where they are joined by Henriquez, Lilla, and an ancient lady, Lilla's aunt. Victoria now almost daily meets Zofloya in secret, and soon her whole heart " is given up to anarchy and crime." The Moor becomes her master and tutor, and by his agency she administers a swift poison to the aunt of Lilla and to Berenza, both of whom expire in agony. The two confederates then seize Lilla herself and imprison the weeping maiden in a mysterious cavern. Henriquez, despairing at her loss, falls ill, but Victoria has recourse to a philtre, brewed by Zofloya, which causes the sick man to believe her Lilla, and after a wild revel he embraces her as his bride. In the morning he awakes to find that Victoria is the partner of his bed. The situation here is not unlike that of Syphax and Erictho in Marston's *Sophonisba*, Acts IV.–V., where the Libyan king is cheated by the witch in Sophonisba's shape, but at dawn she starts up in her own foul hideousness.[1] Henriquez, upon discovering the trick, promptly plunges a sword into his breast and expires. Victoria, mad with rage, rushes to the cave where Lilla is chained, and after a terrible struggle stabs her to death, hurling the body over the cliff. The Moor rebukes her violence, and informs her that suspicion having been aroused, some of her servants are gone to Venice to fetch magistrates and guards, whilst the rest remain to prevent her escape. Zofloya adds, moreover, that he can only save her from arrest and execution if she will give herself wholly to him. This she vows to do, and immediately she falls into a magic slumber. On awaking she finds herself amid mountains and beetling crags ; thunder is bellowing in the valleys, and the red lightning blazes through the sky. The Moor is at her side, and informs her they are in

---

[1] Cf. Settle's *The Female Prelate*, where Pope Joan, feigning to be Angelina, shares the bed of the Duke of Saxony. A fire breaks out and the imposture is exposed.

the heart of the Alps. Banditti surround them, and lead them to a cave where a number of Transpontine brigands are assembled at a feaſt. Their captain, who is masked, asks Zofloya if Victoria is his wife or his miſtress? "Neither," replies the Moor, "yet she is bound to me by indissoluble bands for all eternity." That night Victoria has a vision of a glorious angel who bids her repent and fly from the Moor, since he is not what he seems. When she opens her eyes Zofloya is at her side, and eagerly he asks if she wishes to leave him. She clings to him, vowing in passionate terms to be his for ever. Anon the brigands bring back two prisoners, a man and a wounded woman. The captain of the band cuts down the man remorselessly, and then, throwing aside his mask, shows the features of Leonardo. The woman is his mother, his victim Count Adolphus. Laurina dies, and Leonardo weeps at her death-bed, but Victoria mocks and reviles. Eventually the banditti are betrayed to the soldiers by one of their number, Ginotti. Leonardo falls fighting, and Megalina Strozzi, who has shared his wild career, ſtabs herself to the heart. Victoria and Zofloya are surrounded, but he promises to help her even then if she will once more vow to be his and his alone. When she pronounces the words she immediately finds herself on the summit of a precipitous gorge, alone with the Moor, who suddenly changes from a comely youth to a frightful fiend. "'Behold me as I am, no longer that which I appeared to be, but the sworn enemy of all created nature, by men called Satan. Yes, it was I that under semblance of the Moor appeared to thee.' As he spoke, he grasped more firmly the neck of Victoria, with one push he whirled her headlong down the dreadful abyss!—as she fell his loud dæmonic laugh, his yells of triumph, echoed in her ears; and a mangled corpse she fell, she was received into the foaming waters below."

It will be noticed that this conclusion, though indeed by no means so ſtriking and forceful, is exactly similar to the final scene in Lewis' moſt famous romance where the exulting demon hurls headlong the wretched Ambrosio, who has juſt pledged himself to Lucifer, from the cliff to the water's brink, and presently the swollen ſtream carries "into the river the corse of the despairing monk." As has before been noticed, not only here but throughout *Zofloya* we have incessant and unashamed imitation of *The Monk*. Perhaps with one or two very patent exceptions it was not so much actual incident that Charlotte

E.P.

Dacre pilfered for her pages, as sentiment, characterization, scenic description—though in this particular Mrs. Radcliffe also is laid under wholesale contribution—nomenclature, and a certain lax morality which becomes insufferably trite because palpably a pose and assumed. All these gusts of fierce passion, these pangs and ecstasies of unhallowed love, ring false, and amours which are no doubt intended to convey the sentimental seductiveness of Ovid's poisoned honey seem faded and have lost their fire. These unreal erotics are by no means peculiar to Charlotte Dacre, for a dozen other writers of the school which all too closely imitated "the style of the first edition of *The Monk*" have spiced their churchyard chapters with would-be luscious description, and stand convicted of a conventional and frigid lasciviousness. They blunder with the clumsy and ill-acted impudence of a naturally modest man.

There appears in *Zofloya* a blemish, which it must be confessed is avoided by most romantic writers of the time, and into which no story-teller of practised skill should suffer himself to fall. Charlotte Dacre cannot refrain from frequent and overt allusions to the mystery that surrounds the Moor ; she unduly emphasizes his supernatural power, his gigantic stature, the awful swiftness of his movements from place to place, and far too prematurely does she insist upon the unhallowed alliance he forms with the abandoned Victoria, who again and again in the course of the romance is made to devote herself with horrid vows to her tutor in evil, and swear to be his body and soul through all eternity. It is hardly with surprise we learn in the final scene that Zofloya is " a frightful fiend from the nethermost hell." He was, no doubt, in some sort intended to be a counter-part of Matilda in *The Monk*. But it is to be observed that the figure of the voluptuous beauty whose wanton charms bring about the downfall of Ambrosio, although it has vitality, is quite incongruous and has no consistency. The fact is that Lewis during the course of his narrative changed his mind as to her person and her influence. In the earlier chapters she is a lovely and passionate woman, essentially human, who has become deeply enamoured of the abbot, and who, as she relates in detail, forms a very subtle plan to enter the cloister in order that she may seduce him to her arms, a design which is crowned by nights of unbridled venery. She does not shrink from the practices of black magic and sells herself to the demon. In the final scene where Lucifer is hideously exulting over the lost Ambrosio he cries : " I observed your blind idolatry of the Madonna's picture. I bade a subordinate but crafty spirit assume a similar form, and you eagerly yielded to the blandishments of Matilda." So the character which commences as a maiden torn with desire ends as a succubus. This is a bad fault, but it passes well-nigh unnoticed in the calenture of this fevered romance.

Zofloya achieved an immense success, and in August, 1810, it was epitomized in a chap-book of twenty-eight pages as *The Dæmon of Venice, An Original Romance,* " By a Lady." This abridgement, published by Thomas Tegg, 3, Cheapside, a well-known purveyor of cheap novels and smaller literary ware, is embellished with two most appropriate illustrations, wherein, as in the Primrose family group, the painter has not been sparing of his colours. Such an issue proves the popularity of the work, and was no doubt contraband, as not only is the title altered, but the characters are further disguised, Victoria di Loredani becoming Arabella di Lenardi ; Leonardo, Orlando ; Adolphus, Jaques ; la signora de Modena, Signora di Tabitha ; Berenza, Amiens ; Lilla, Agnes ; Henriquez, Francisco ; and Zofloya, Abdullah the Moor.

Particularly interesting is the connexion between *Zofloya* and Shelley's two juvenile romances *Zastrozzi* (1810) and *St. Irvyne, or The Rosicrucian* (1811). Crude and exaggerated as these novels may be, they are important in that they already foreshadow much of the poet's later self and they clearly contain the embryo of that philosophy which found immortal expression in his greatest poems. Medwin, who tells us that *The Italian* was a favourite work of Shelley's youth, goes on to say that *Zofloya* " quite enraptured " the young enthusiast, and hence it was the source for his two romances. It must be remembered too that Godwin's *St. Leon* was ever in Shelley's hands, and he mentioned to Stockdale that it had powerfully influenced him in writing *St. Irvyne*. It would be easy to show in detail how amply Shelley drew from Mrs. Dacre—more than one passage is actually paraphrased—but it must suffice to touch upon but a few points. In *Zastrozzi* Matilda di Laurentini—Matilda is from *The Monk* and Laurentini from *The Mysteries of Udolpho*—is a close replica of Victoria di Loredani, and the scene where Henriquez or Verezzi is seduced, or well-nigh seduced, by a medicated philtre occurs in both novels, Lilla being named Julia by Shelley. Incidentally there is a character Verezzi in *The Mysteries of Udolpho*. In *St. Irvyne* Megalena has been borrowed from Megalena Strozzi in *Zofloya*, whence Shelley has also taken his Alpine bandits wholesale. The name Cavigni (*St. Irvyne*) is from *The Mysteries of Udolpho*. Ginotti of the "strangely and fearfully gleaming eyeball" has his name from Mrs. Dacre's brigand, who betrays the robbers' lair on Mt. Cenis to the Duke of Savoy. Further comparison were needless, but it should not be forgotten that at Christmas, 1809–1810, was being composed *Original Poetry by Victor and Cazire*, which latter name is that of the heroine of *The Confessions of the Nun of St. Omer*.

Mrs. Dacre's third romance, *The Libertine*, which appeared in April, 1807, achieved a popularity almost equal to that of her famous *Zofloya*, and was discussed on every side. Montmorency and his daughter, Gabrielle, have retired from a troublous world to an Arcadian valley in Switzerland, "that sublimely beautiful part which the magic pen of the tender enthusiast Rousseau has rescued from obscurity." During a terrific storm Count Angelo d'Albini seeks shelter at their house, where Montmorency was reading, but not aloud, the "Maxims of La Rochefoucalt." The visitor so charms his host by his noble bearing and courtly manners that he is pressed to stay for a few days, during which time he promptly seduces the unsophisticated but pliant Gabrielle, who, however, does not forsake her father's roof as her lover suggests, whereupon he is quick to take his leave. In due course Gabrielle becomes a mother, and Montmorency dies broken-hearted at his daughter's shame. She then resolves to follow her faithless Angelo, and entrusting her babe to the care of some honest cottagers, she dons male attire—an episode which reminds one of the Elizabethan dramatists—and calling herself Eugene makes her way to Naples. Here she enters the service of the Count, who confides to his page that he has a mistress, Oriana, "a bewitching Genoese." Bravoes presently appear on the scene, and in a scuffle Eugene is wounded, thus saving the unworthy Angelo's life. She is recognized and greeted with rapture, being installed in his mansion. In a few months, however, the fickle wretch again deserts her and goes to England. Gabrielle follows him to London, bringing with her their little son Felix. Milborough, a treacherous waiting-maid, who seems modelled upon Millwood in Lillo's *The London Merchant*

(*George Barnwell*), attends Gabrielle. Angelo, who is attracted by this woman's charms, intrigues with her, but he is fast reducing himself to poverty by gaming and other extravagances. Guessing that the end cannot be far, Milborough, robbing him of all upon which she can lay hands, disappears, taking with her the child whom she has already begun to initiate into every wickedness. Angelo is completely ruined, and only the patient Gabrielle clings to him in his misfortunes. They are reduced to great distress, which is unexpectedly relieved by one Ellesmere, a former friend, who now restores large sums of money of which he cheated him. At last Angelo makes Gabrielle his wife, but owing to her privations and sorrow she dies on the threshold of happier days. The widower goes to Paris, and here he is taken to a luxurious house filled with a superb company. To his surprise he recognizes in the hostess Milborough. This fair cyprian informs him that Felix has been stolen from her by a woman who seems to have taken a lesson from her own conduct and decamped with a large casket of jewels, money, and the boy, who cannot be traced. In horror Angelo flies from cities to seek a country retreat. He encounters a maiden Ida, who is living in a delicious rural solitude. Struck by her beauty, he wooes her. It appears that she has been betrayed by one Darlowitz, and later he finds that she is his daughter, Agnes. She enters a convent of the strictest order, and Angelo hurries back to England. On passing through Paris he learns that Milborough, owing to her riot and debauchery, has gone mad and is the hopeless inmate of an asylum for the most violently distempered and incurable lunatics. Arriving in England he settles down to a life of retirement and regret. One night he is attacked by a highwayman, to whom he gives all his gold. The robber is shortly afterwards taken, and when Angelo attends the trial, to his horror, he recognizes the prisoner as his son. Felix is condemned to death, and the wretched father shoots himself at the hour of execution.

Although a novel of many and complicated incidents and adventures must be sadly impaired by so brief a recapitulation, it is to be hoped that even this bald narrative may convey some idea of this powerful and distressing story, which fully deserved the success it immediately enjoyed, for by 1807 it had run into a third edition. It will be noticed that some hints are derived from *The Monk*, and Lewis no doubt suggested the horror of incest, which also appears in Walpole's *The Mysterious Mother*, printed at Strawberry Hill, 1768, and Shelley's *The Cenci*, 1819.

The Libertine was turned into French by Elisabeth de Bon, a famous purveyor of melodramatic fiction, and the translator in 1815 of Anna Maria Porter's *The Recluse of Norway*, 4 vols., 1814, together with many other novels of the same school. *Angelo, Comte d'Albini, ou Les Dangers du Vice*, "par Charlotte Dacre connue sous le nom de Rosa Matilda," was published at Paris, 3 vols., 1816, "chez Arthur Bertrand," and was soon to be seen in every fashionable boudoir and ruelle.

The story of *The Passion* is told in epistolary fashion, a series of letters mainly between Count Wiemar and Baron Rozendorf, or Rozendorf and Darlowitz. Perhaps there is no little truth in the harsh remarks of *The Critical Review*, December, 1811 : "The inflated extravagance of diction, which deforms Rosa Matilda's novel of 'The Passions,' deducts very much from the interest which her work would otherwise have excited. The effect of her talents, for talents she undoubtedly possesses, is impaired by the repulsive affectation of her style." At any rate Count Wiemar, who somewhat vaguely heads his first effusion Switzerland, where "it is nothing uncommon to see a herdsman with a volume of Voltaire or Rosseau [*sic*] in his hand," which is, to say the least, extremely regrettable, protests to his friend that "I would not for the treasures of the east undergo another year such as the last I spent at Vienna." Here he seems to have engaged the affections of the Countess Appollonia Zulmer, whom, however, he did not wish to lead to the altar, a feeling Rozendorf highly approves, since the lady "cannot breathe out of the warm meridian of gallantry and universal admiration." In a letter to her gouvernante, Madame de Hauteville, the imperious Appollonia declares her frantic love for the fascinating Wiemar. Unfortunately she is in the power of two blackmailers, Pietro Mondovi and Catherine Glatz, who are continually draining her of large sums. We now have a letter to Rozendorf from Wiemar, who is at Zurich. He has fallen in love with Julia de Montalban, who resides with her mother in a small cottage, and he soon discovers that "they are supposed to be persons of rank, driven by misfortune into this seclusion ; that they have already resided here several years, and are highly respected by the few with whom they deign to associate," all of which seems pretty clearly taken from *The Italian*, when Ellena is living in great retirement near

Naples with Signora Bianchi. The letters now cease, and a brief note informs us that Wiemar weds Julia de Montalban, upon the death of whose mother after four years they return to Vienna. The Countess Zulmer instantly seeks their society, and before long becomes " almost the shadow of the Countess Wiemar," whom she endeavours to corrupt by a course of insidious reading and false philosophy. But presently she is withdrawn from these temptations, as Count Wiemar takes his wife and children to visit his dear friend Count Darlowitz, the spouse of the amiable Amelia. It is soon apparent, however, that Darlowitz is fast falling in love with Julia, and before long, although she cries, "The hot blush of agonizing shame tingles on my burning cheek," it is pretty plain that the lady returns his passion. This she very unwisely confesses in a letter to Appollonia Zulmer, who, of course, promptly persuades her not to resist. " I am a fatuist, Julia," writes the lady, by which she probably means a fatalist, " and I believe the pictured web of our lives is woven by the hand of destiny, and you, too, must yield to this doctrine of fatality, of which you are so reluctant a victim." Meanwhile Amelia has expressed a wish that her husband shall take her to visit her mother, the Duchess of Sternach, who resides at Naples, and Wiemar resolves that he and Julia shall join the party, whence the two lovers are constantly thrown in one another's company. Appollonia now employs Mondovi to convey a letter to Wiemar at Naples, wherein, under a feigned hand, she more than hints at the state of affairs. Rozendorf upon learning this writes a stern letter to Darlowitz, bidding him " *save from deep perdition the object of your guilty passion.*" He also addresses some very plain speaking to the Countess Zulmer, whose Machiavellian guile has, he is confident, dealt the blow. Darlowitz on finding that his secret is " in the possession of *another !* " gives way to frenzy. He dare not think that his " Angel of innocence, pure as spiritual æther," should be suspected, his " sublimated hopes " destroyed. In fact his emotions are so fearful that a fever supervenes, and he is only recalled from death's door by Julia's confession of love. The situation is exceedingly poignant, and in spite of some stilted phraseology it is exceedingly well portrayed. In the letters which pass between Darlowitz and Julia Mrs. Dacre shows herself possessed of considerable power and imagination. An accident reveals the state of her husband's affections to Amelia, whose broken heart cannot survive the shock. Although

written in too florid a style to be truly pathetic, an emotion
above all demanding the utmost simplicity, it cannot be denied
that some passages of the death-bed scene, which is not unduly
prolonged, are extremely moving.   Julia flies, and Darlowitz,
in agonies of remorse, destroys himself by his own hand.
Unfortunately the wretched wife seeks a refuge with the Countess
Zulmer, and writing from Zurich to implore her compassion,
receives in reply a letter of biting irony which concludes in a
whirl of passion : " Now then, let the mask be torn off. . . .
Learn, too, that you have been my tool !—my puppet !—the
instrument of my revenge on the perfidious Wiemar, who loved
me ere he knew you—the object of it yourself, for daring to
possess a heart which had wrested itself from me, and which, but
for the intervention of your accursed influence, I might still have
regained."   The triumphant Medea writes in similar strain to
Wiemar.   Meanwhile, in order to escape the increasing extortions
of Mondovi, she secretly plans to leave Vienna, taking with her all
her jewels and gold.   Mondovi, however, discovers her design
and, disguising himself as a postilion, drives her coach into the
Black Forest, where he descends, drags her forth, and pierces
her with deadly wounds, whilst a confederate rifles the chaise.
At this moment Rozendorf and his servants, on their way to join
Wiemar, rush up, attracted by the shrieks of the wretched woman.
They rescue her, disarming the ruffians, and carry her to a
wayside inn, where she expires in terrible agonies of mind and
body.   It is discovered that Julia has taken refuge with some
cottagers at a hamlet named Eglisaw, but in consequence of the
fatal events in which she was involved her reason has well-nigh
forsaken her.   Curiously enough, towards the conclusion of
the story the epistolary form is dropped, and the events which
follow are now simply narrated.   Wiemar passes several months
of great unhappiness, for it is felt that if he presents himself to
his sorrowing wife her fear and remorse may drive her to
frantic madness.   In fact she has already possessed herself of a
penknife belonging to her attendant Jeannette, but this she is
unable to use.   The end comes when one winter's night the
wretched maniac, tortured to frenzy by her self-accusations of
murder and unfaith, escapes from the house and, after wandering
far and wide in the storm, chances upon the path leading to the
cottage where she once dwelt in happiness with her mother, and
where now her husband is sojourning to watch over her as best

he may. " She draws near! nearer and nearer still; her strength fails, her fainting footsteps flag; yet she gains the winding avenue which leads to the house; she beholds the very door! A hollow cry escapes her, and with a frightful effort she drags herself along; a few steps more, and she touches the threshold." But just as she is about to knock feebly for admittance her strength fails, and she falls without a sound, whilst the heavy snowflakes wind a soft white pall over her dead body.

I am very well aware that any analysis of a novel is apt to be bald and commonplace; in a mere relation of incidents much that is of interest evaporates completely. The art of the writer fades away, and dry bare bones alone are left, nor is there any prophet to clothe them with flesh. No doubt the account I have endeavoured to give of Charlotte Dacre's romances is trite, but yet I did not very well see how otherwise it was possible to review briefly these works, which had in their own day no inconsiderable meed of popularity. It is, I venture to think, good sometimes to turn from the great ones of literature and adventure among the smaller names. When I first read *English Bards and Scotch Reviewers* I was full of curiosity concerning " the lovely Rosa," and my curiosity went unsatisfied, for I was never able to find anyone then or in after years who had so much as heard of the lady. I determined to explore. I have always had a love for the occult, and I suppose there are but few, if any, writers in English fiction whose works are more difficult to discover than are the romances of Charlotte Dacre, " better known by the Name of *Rosa Matilda*," who married Byrne of the " Morning Post."

THE MARQUIS DE SADE

A STUDY IN ALGOLAGNIA

THE MARQUIS DE SADE

A STUDY IN ALGOLAGNIA

IN the volume of autobiographical reminiscences, published
posthumously, to which Henry James had given the title *The
Middle Years*, there is related an incident that is at once illuminating and instructive. The great novelist tells how, on a
certain occasion whilst lunching at Aldworth with the Tenny-
sons, Mrs. Greville, who was of the party, happened to mention
in some connexion one of her French relatives, Mademoiselle
Laure de Sade. The name, James candidly confesses, fell on his
own ear " with a certain effect of unconscious provocation ; but,"
he continues, " this was as nothing compared to the effect on the
ear of our host. ' De Sade ! ' he at once exclaimed with interest,
and with the consequence, I may frankly add, of my wondering
almost to ecstasy, that is to the ecstasy of curiosity, to what length
he would proceed. He proceeded admirably—admirably for the
triumph of simplification—to the very greatest length imaginable,
as was signally promoted by the fact that clearly no one present,
with a single exception, recognized the name or the nature of the
scandalous, the long ignored, the at last all but unnameable
author ; least of all the gentle relative of Mademoiselle Laure,
who listened with the blankest grace to her friend's enumeration
of his titles to infamy, among which that of his most notorious
work was pronounced. It was the homeliest, frankest, most
domestic passage, as who should say, and most remarkable for
leaving none of us, save myself, by my impression, in the least
embarrassed or bewildered ; largely, I think, because of the failure
—a failure the most charmingly flat—of all measure on the part
of the auditors and speaker alike of what might be intended or
understood, of what, in fine, the latter was talking about. He
struck me in truth as neither knowing nor communicating knowledge. . . ."

The myopic attitude of Tennyson, which is so admirably
summed up by Henry James in that last penetrating phrase, has

been with some noteworthy exceptions, the severely conventional attitude of all who have had occasion to deal with the Marquis de Sade. Where possible he has been tacitly ignored ; but when it was inevitable that his name should be mentioned, he has been uniformly covered with excess of obloquy and abuse by those who neither knew nor could communicate knowledge, who never read a word of his writings nor troubled to comprehend the smallest fragment of his philosophy ; but were doltishly content to boom on, emptily enumerating his titles to infamy, and, above all, never forgetting to vociferate the name of his most notorious romance.

And yet de Sade was a writer, a critic, and a philosopher of no mean order. His works contain, it is true, much that is extravagant, much that is diffuse, much that is fantastically erotic, but in spite of all his faults and impudicities, he remains a figure of vital interest, and surely as such may be impartially and dispassionately considered without any palliative condonation of his obscenity or necessary embracing of his philosophical ideas. To students of sexual psychology he is undeniably of prime importance. For, deservedly or no, as the case may be, it is his name that has been given to an impulse, which in a more or less marked degree, is, in the words of the greatest living authority, " one of the most difficult problems, and yet one of the most fundamental, in the whole range of sexual psychology "—the relationship of love to pain.

Iwan Bloch once went so far as to say that the Marquis de Sade was the first to realize the immense importance of the sexual question, a statement which it were perhaps unwise actually to adopt, for as Dr. Havelock Ellis, commenting on this, acutely remarks in a private letter to myself, " the sexual question " is a vague phrase. None the less it is eminently striking that so expert an authority as Bloch can have advanced such a claim. But in this connexion we must not forget the gigantic work of the moral theologians, of whom many of the greatest names, Antonio Diana, Caramuel, de Sa, Sanchez, Tamburini, and a score beside, flourished during the sixteenth and seventeenth centuries. Concerning these Bloch, in The Sexual Life of Our Time, very justly affirms : " There is not a single sexual problem that has not been discussed in the most subtle manner by the theological casuists . . . even the most improbable and impossible."

De Sade was essentially a pioneer, and to quote the almost

impeccable judgement of Dr. Havelock Ellis : " He considerably furthered the progress of knowledge in the field of sex by his serious and precise attitude toward sexual aberrations."

Donatien-Alphonse-François, Marquis de Sade,[1] was born on the 2nd June, 1740, at Paris, in the house of the great Conde. He belonged to a very noble, ancient, and distinguished Provençal family ; the founder of which, Bertrand, who derived his name from the little village of Saze near Avignon, is spoken of by Cæsar de Nostre Dame in his mediæval *Chronicles of Provence* as having been summoned to a conclave of nobles held at Arles in 1216. A century later, on Monday in Holy week, April 6th, 1327, the wife of Hugues de Sade, Madonna Laura, when at her devotions in the church of S. Clare at Avignon was seen and thenceforth adored with passionate worship by Francis Petrarch, " the Laureate Poete," who has immortalized her in the sweetest ecstasy of Italian song. And so the history of literature by some strange caprice has united in the same family a dame, " ensky'd and sainted," the sublime inspiration of the mystic enthusiast of chivalrous love, and a writer whose name is commonly even more notorious than that of Venetian Aretine for the wayward license of his pages, the audacity of his philosophy, his unflinching concentration upon the problems and byways, the aberrations and pathology of sex.

It is noticeable that not a few members of the proud line of de Sade were distinguished in literature, above all Jacques Paul de Sade, the uncle of the Marquis, vicar-general of the archdioceses of Toulouse and Narbonne, who, after having basked long in the smiles of Madame de la Popelinière and passed many a gay and frivolous year at Paris in the hey-day of the reign of Louis XV, eventually retired to Vaucluse, and devoted his time to compiling *The Memoirs of Francis Petrarch* (1764), a work which for its unwearied research and expert scholarship is even to-day held in esteem by all serious students of the great Italian Poet. There can be little doubt that the Marquis de Sade inherited many of the qualities of his uncle, who, renowned during youth for his gallantries and intrigues, in later life became so wholly absorbed in literature. The Marquis shows the keenest appreciation of poetry, and in more than one passage he has testified to his

---

[1] This was his title as eldest son. Upon the death of his father he became Comte de Sade, but he is always spoken and written of as Marquis, and it would be worse than pedantry to attempt an alteration.

especial admiration for Petrarch, whom he terms "a charming poet," and "the sweet singer of Vaucluse."

The early life of the Marquis de Sade he has sketched for us himself in the autobiographical "Histoire de Valcour," letter five of the epistolary romance *Aline et Valcour*. "I was born and brought up," he writes, "in the palace of a great and noble prince, to whose house my mother had the honour to belong, and who was moreover about my own age. In these circumstances it was impressed upon me that I must gain his goodwill, in order that having enjoyed his friendship from childhood, I might count on his help and influence my whole life long. But my natural vanity would have nothing of it." Indeed during some boyish squabble over the result of a nursery game the two little lads fell to fisticuffs and could only be separated by force. Thereupon the Marquis was promptly packed off to his grandmother in the country ; but, as he frankly avows, her devoted affection only served to foster his faults and develop his overweening pride, quick temper, selfishness and aristocratic conceit.

After a short time, however, he exchanged this injudicious petticoat rule for the tutelage of his uncle, the famous litterateur, who personally supervised the boy's lessons, and in 1750 passed him at the age of ten into the Parisian College, Louis-le-Grand, one of the most fashionable and expensive schools of the capital. There he remained for four years. His family had already decided that he must embrace a military career, and accordingly, when scarcely fifteen he was given a commission in the cavalry of the King's Body Guard, the most exclusive regiment of the day, to which influence and rank alone could aspire. "There can be little doubt," notes Dr. Havelock Ellis, "that the experiences of his military life, working on a femininely vicious temperament, had much to do with the development of his perversion." But so extravagant and costly was the mess in this select regiment that after two years de Sade found an opportunity of being transferred into the Burgundian cavalry, and at nineteen he was gazetted as Captain.

There are several descriptions of the young de Sade at this juncture of his life, and although an unimportant detail here and there may differ, all agree that he was remarkably handsome and possessed quite exceptional fascination and personal charm. Octave Uzanne, quoting documentary evidence, presents him as "an adorable youth whose delicately pale and passion-wearied face, lighted up by two large black eyes, already bore the languorous imprint of the vice which was to corrupt his whole being " ; his voice was " soft and gently caressing," his gait " graceful as a woman's." Paul Lacroix spoke of his " oval face, fine curly hair, and magnetic blue eyes." Unfortunately no authentic likeness exists. A bad lithograph printed in 1840 as frontispiece to a catchpenny pamphlet is obviously mere cheap hocus ; the often reproduced medallion, supported by two fauns, is at best a clever pastiche from a composite miniature painted about 1820 ; but a third portrait, engraved by H. Biberstein in 1866, has value from an artistic point of view and corresponds very closely with the description given by Uzanne. It cannot escape notice that both Uzanne and Lacroix, as also the Biberstein picture, delineate a markedly homosexual type, and there can be no doubt that at this period the Marquis de Sade was greatly addicted to passive homosexuality. Upon his return to Paris in the winter of 1762, after he had completed his military service, his father, as we are told by a contemporary, took him severely to task for certain " péchés de jeunesse," and there is no question that in the romance of *Justine* when the young Comte de Brissac, who is represented as completely feminine in temperament, defends and explains his homosexuality, the Marquis is simply speaking through his character. Indeed the details are so intimate, the psychology so true, that only experience or the result of wide scientific research could have supplied them.

Save for the moral theologians whom one can fairly regard as experts, although experts working on academic lines, de Sade is, I think, the first who has dealt with the problem of homosexuality in an intelligent and impartial manner. Fully realizing the immense importance of the psychology of inversion he anticipated the monographs of Karl Heinrich Ulrichs by three quarters of a century, and we find in his pages many of the arguments and most of the conclusions of the famous Hanoverian jurist. It is true that one of his favourite theories, " anima muliebris uirili corpore inclusa," the very formula of Ulrichs himself, cannot in the light of more recent investigation be loosely accepted, although it is still repeated as by Dr. William J. Robinson in his *Treatment of Sexual Impotence* (1917), when he writes : " The homosexual man means a being with the body of a man but with the soul or sex instinct of a woman." However we know that the problem is far more complex than this. Homosexuality is essentially of the brain not merely of the body, and this is recognized by S. Thomas in the *Summa*, when he defines it as " affectus," a technical medical term, which Quintilian translates by the Greek ἠθος. De Brissac in *Justine* avers that he has all the emotions and desires of a woman ; he is Ulrichs' " Weibling," a type not uncommon among young homosexuals, and occasionally accentuated by them owing to their deliberate fashion of dress, gait, coiffure, and voice. But here we must guard against the vulgar error which still persists, and it is still useful to controvert and deny, namely, that these manners are in any way genuinely characteristic of Uranians. Such affectations are indulged in only by a small number, and by most of these because they suppose their effeminacy will attract their fellows. But many who are temperamentally feminine are careful to differ in no marked detail of appearance or wardrobe from the ordinary individual. Moreover we often find that a homosexual of pronounced womanish habits loses these when he has passed his first youth, although the womanly emotions, tact, gentleness, persist.

To-day, the line of argument de Sade uses with reference to homosexuality naturally seems a little obvious, but I would point out it has only become so in the last five and twenty years. The position he maintains has been in the aggregate accepted by all psychologists, sex authorities, and ethical scientists of note. But his ideas which he poured forth in somewhat fervid and impassioned rhetoric needed restating in scientific terms, cold, inevitably logical, crystallized. His arguments required to be reinforced, to be expanded, to receive new balance and weight from medical and social investigation ; and it is interesting to notice that in the monumental work of those two supreme masters, Magnus Hirschfeld and Havelock Ellis, amongst their mass of cumulative evidence, but restated, clarified, added to, we find those very arguments which were put forward by de Sade.

It may not be impertinent very briefly to indicate here the line he adopts in *La Philosophie dans le Boudoir* (1795). He first disposes of that absurd misnomer " unnatural " ; next he proceeds to demonstrate the impossibility of a famous legend in early Hebrew folk lore, the destruction of Sodom and Gomorrah, that wicked myth which has been productive of untold misery and mischief. At considerable length he combats the feeble position assumed by those who would seek to argue from the

premise that homosexuality is unprocreative, and incidentally
he points out that fertile nature destroys as well as constructs.
Finally with the aid of salient examples he shows that homosexuality " has been present in all ages and places throughout
the Old World and the New," "semper, et ubique, et ab
omnibus."

There can be no doubt that de Sade's father was greatly
disturbed by the current reports of his son's indiscretions, which
indeed seem to have been pretty freely circulated, and so to
counteract these he selected a bride for the overgay young soldier.
A friend of many years' standing, M. de Montreuil, President of
the Auxiliary Court at Paris, had two daughters, one aged twenty,
and the other thirteen. Both were beautiful ; the eldest, Renée-
Pélagie, being a majestic brunette of a sincerely religious mind ;
whilst the youngest, Louise, had fair fleecy hair, limpid blue eyes,
and a passionate southern nature. It had already been decided by
the four parents that the Marquis should marry the eldest, but, as it
chanced, when he visited the house she was unwell, and he only
met Louise. With her he fell violently in love at first sight, and
throughout the years his adoration never wavered nor waned.
His love was reciprocated with equal flame. The consequence
proved that upon seeing Renée he could scarcely conceal his
dislike, and he forthwith begged M. de Montreuil to allow him
to make Louise his wife. The President curtly refused, and
Madame de Montreuil, a woman of the haughtiest and most
inflexible character, at once placed Louise in a distant convent
the name of which was never divulged. Under great family
pressure, and with many a sad protest, the Marquis at length
reluctantly consented to become the husband of Mdlle. de
Montreuil, and the marriage was solemnized with much magni-
ficence at S. Roch, May 17th, 1763. De Sade's wife loved him
dearly and in spite of every neglect clung to him and served his
interests with the tenderest devotion. Her reward was repulsion,
contempt, suspicion, and mistrust. He looked upon her as
the fatal obstacle to his happiness, and in order to fly her, in
order to forget his own hopeless misery, he flung himself headlong into an abyss of wildest profligacy and cloyed his senses
with every excess. But as Dr. Havelock Ellis says : " He was,
however, always something of an artist, something of a student,
something of a philosopher."

De Sade was already predisposed by heredity to emotional

extremes ; he was markedly influenced by his environment ; and when he was not only deprived of the woman he loved, but compelled to enter into a union with her sister whom he loathed, his agonies of relentless craving and despair acting upon strong sexual instincts unbalanced his cooler judgment and were indubitably the cause of that unrestrained and sinister eroticism which is so prominent a feature of his writings.

He was sprung from a long and effete line of ancestors, of whom some such as the Bishop of Cavaillon, and his own father, the Comte de Sade, were men of austere and religious lives ; others, such as the old Provençal nobles and the friend of Voltaire, were rakes of the first water ; whilst, as we have seen, his uncle, Paul de Sade, in youth a gay gallant, in later years became an exemplary scholar and litterateur. Not a few members of this ancient house were noted for their profligacy, or their saintliness, as the case might be.

Again, the Marquis de Sade whilst yet a mere lad, had been thrown into the dissolute society of the officers of the smartest regiment in the French Army, and even in his teens he became intimately acquainted with all the licentiousness of military life. Nor did these lessons fall on unfruitful soil.

Moreover, a French nobleman living at Paris in the reign of Louis XV could not lack ample opportunity for pleasure. Hegel, in his *Philosophy of History*, thus characterizes the period :— " The whole situation in France is an extraordinary compound of licence and privileges resting on no sound basis but contrary to every rule of right reason, a state of chaotic sentiments and ideas, accompanied by the utmost depravity of morals—it is the reign of iniquity incarnate, which before the conscience of the nation is rudely aroused has lost all sense of shame and is utterly unabashed in its effrontery and open impudence." It was indeed an hour of utter corruption—social, political, moral, and not before the kingdom had passed into the melting pot of the French Revolution could it hope for the dawn of a better day. Tyranny, oppression of the poor, profiteering, inhumanity, the most hideous cruelty, were rampant on every side. One could have seen

> " . . . Corruption boil and bubble
> Till it o'er-run the stew : laws for all faults,
> But faults so countenanc'd that the strong statutes
> [Stood] As much in mock as mark."

A peer or a rich man need never be afraid of legal process save haply he offended someone greater or wealthier than himself. Occasionally indeed by some untoward accident a scandal of more than ordinary vileness would evade all attempts to stifle it, whereupon the authorities, half-heartedly enough, but with a loud blare of moral trumpets, would attempt some spasmodic effort in the wrong direction. The frank venality of politicians and officials could perhaps only be paralleled in the history of our own times.

The eighteenth century was pre-eminently the century of systematized and studied licentiousness. De Sade himself in *Justine*, pronounces it to be corrupt to the core, and adds that it is not merely difficult but even dangerous to attempt to set up for virtue in such a milieu. All social life was concentrated on the elegant accomplishment of the sexual act. Science, art, literature, fashion, conversation, lent their every aid to enhance and embellish physical desire. " Pleasure, voluptuous pleasure, was the soul of the eighteenth century," cries de Goncourt. Phallic ecstasy almost became a religion as in the days of decadent Rome. It was an era of subtle artificiality, of powder and patches, silk and perfume, when the silken petticoat, the lace ruffle and essenced hair proved more provocative by candlelight than clean nudity in the golden noontide sun. Society seemed infected with a general satyriasis, and men worshipped indifferently at the shrines of the Marquise de Pompadour, "maman Putain " ; or le petit Fleury, a young actor, on whom the Venetian Ambassador had settled an annual income of eight thousand pounds.

It is often said that " great men are the product of their age," and the remarkable figure of the Marquis de Sade was essentially the complete product of his time. For the seventeenth century in France, besides being, as we have shown, an epoch of the frankest and most unrestrained licence, was also marked by rapine, deeds of violence and judicial cruelties that almost exceed belief. In Paris, robberies, burglaries, assassinations, murderous assaults, were of daily occurrence, and hardly excited remark ; at nightfall gangs of armed thieves patrolled the streets, and sometimes even openly attacked houses and shops. The roads were infested with highwaymen in every direction, and it was no infrequent thing for an organized band of brigands to penetrate the suburbs of country towns, to burn, pillage, and destroy in all directions.

Public executions were prolonged with every variety of torture. Beheading was almost unknown ; the ordinary punishment was the wheel, on which the unfortunate wretch would linger for hours with crushed limbs, whilst huge crowds gloated over his anguish. The execution of Damiens, who, for attempting the life of Louis XV, was put to death, January 5th, 1757, amid tortures of the most fiendish cruelty, passed into a proverb as did the similar fate of Balthazar Gerard two centuries before.[1] A vast mob assembled to watch the agonies of Damiens, which are too hideous for description, and every window overlooking the Place de Grève, nay, the very roofs and parapets, were let at enormous prices. It has been well said that a thousand executions by the guillotine could not atone for this horror. Casanova relates an extraordinary anecdote of the voluptuousness of three women who were absorbed spectators. The most sinister and sanguinary pages of de Sade are baby tales compared to fact.

De Sade soon achieved a peculiar reputation even amid the Parisian Saturnalia. It was bruited that his " petite maison " at Arcueil was the scene of more than ordinarily reckless debauchery.

The phrase, " petite maison," had at this period a very special connotation which it may be well to explain.

Under the august rule of Mde. de Maintenon, the Court of Louis XIV had outwardly assumed the most rigid etiquette and decorum, and a strict morality was enforced which compelled the younger noblemen to seek their pleasures clandestinely at a distance. Hence the custom generally arose of purchasing a cottage, a truly rustic cabin, on the very outskirts of Paris, or in some neighbouring village, where the duke or marquis, sick of the restraints and rules of the entourage of the old King, might entertain his mistress and intrigue as he would. In order to obtain greater freedom and escape recognition, the gallants were wont to assume the attire of a peasant, or at least of a small shopkeeper. For a few hours the change to lowly lodging and plain fare was no doubt amusing and enjoyable enough. After

---

[1] Damiens is referred to by Goldsmith in *The Traveller*. For an allusion to Balthazar Gerard see Fletcher's *The Woman's Prize*, Act II, 2, which, after some trouble with the censor, Sir Henry Herbert, was given at S. James' on November 28th. 1633, before Charles I and his queen, and " Very well lik't." It was regarded as an old play, and must have been originally produced several years before. On October 18th, 1633, Herbert sent for the book and forbade a performance of the play. On October 21st he returned the script " purgd of oaths, prophaness, and ribaldrye."

a while it came to be generally recognized that these little establishments were obviously favourable to assignations of all kinds, and they quickly loſt their Arcadian simplicity. In the less frequented suburbs, houses surrounded by large gardens were chosen and commodiously furnished. The Comte d'Evreux and the Duc de Richelieu set the fashion, and a few years later there was not a man with any pretence to ſtyle or manners who had not his " petite maison " in some quarter of Paris.

In the days of Louis XV the " petites maisons," ſtill preserving as far as possible their gardens and ruſtic frontage, became Cyprian temples. Often the moſt celebrated architeſts of the time had almoſt entirely rebuilt the interior ; the decorations were by Boucher, Fragonard, Columbiani, Zucchi and Watteau ; Heppelwhite and Chippendale designed the furniture. Nor was there even lacking a little library of amatoria, the verses of Grécourt and Alexis Piron, the libertine tales of Crébillon, and the French Aretine. Such was a " petite maison " in the reign of Louis XV.

A few months after his marriage the Marquis de Sade was accused of being concerned at a famous " petite maison " in an orgy which seems for some reason to have caused a grave scandal. The details of this excess are not known, but he was arreſted therefor, and committed to Vincennes. There is extant an intereſting letter dated November 2nd, from the Marquis to the Lieutenant of Police. Herein he vaguely acknowledges certain irregularities, but stoutly denies that he was present at the debauch which had given such public offence. There is a note appended by the Lieutenant to the effeſt that de Sade wished to see the confessor of the Royal Prison, and he asks the prieſt to attend as soon as possible. Meanwhile the family of Madame de Sade urgently petitioned for her husband's release, and in a document of November 4th, an officer of the King's household writes in reply, " His Majeſty does not purpose that M. de Sade shall remain long at Vincennes." A few days afterwards the Marquis was indeed released, but with a ſtriſt order that he should reside away from Paris, and accordingly he was compelled to join his wife at her father's château in Normandy.

To a young man—he was only three and twenty—of the Marquis's taſtes and spirit this exile, which laſted a year, muſt have been intolerable, for it was not until September 11th, 1764, that an order was signed permitting him to return to Paris. There he at once resumed his place in the world of pleasure and fashion.

On the 3rd of April, 1768, the evening of Holy Saturday, the Marquis was crossing the Place des Victoires, when a woman, who appeared young and beautiful, accosted him and asked an alms. He questioned her, and she replied that her name was Rosa Keller, and that she had just been left a widow by a Swiss pastrycook, who died in direst poverty. The Marquis seemed to take an interest in her unhappy state, and, hinting that he was in need of a housekeeper, suggested she should accompany him to his " petite maison." When they had arrived here he showed her all the rooms, and eventually took her up in a garret, where he suddenly produced a pistol and bade her strip off her clothes. In spite of all tears and entreaties he compelled her to submit forthwith to a severe and indecent flagellation, after which he anointed her bruises with a sovereign ointment, and left her, locking the door behind him. The next day he visited her again, and with a small knife inflicted several slight wounds. These he healed with the same unguent as he had previously employed. The terrified woman at length succeeded in unfastening a window whence she flung herself into the street. A crowd promptly collected; information was given to the Lieutenant of Police; and a few hours after the Marquis was arrested. Such is an outline of the affair, which, ten days after it occurred, was detailed by Madame Du Deffand in a letter to Horace Walpole. Writing again on the morrow, April 13th, she further says : " Since yesterday I have learned the rest of the de Sade story. His ' petite maison ' is at Arcueil ; he flagellated and wounded the poor woman on the same occasion, and immediately bathed her stripes and bruises with balsam ; he untied her hands, wrapped her up well in fine linen, and laid her in a good bed. Scarcely was she alone when she made use of the sheets and her stockings to lower herself through the window ; the local magistrate instructed her to carry her plaint direct to the Lieutenant of Police, who thereupon summoned M. de Sade. Far from showing any confusion or shame the Marquis declares he has done a public service by the discovery of an ointment which immediately heals all wounds and wales ; and that was indeed its effect upon this woman. She has not yet decided to prosecute her assailant, but she will more probably demand a sum of money as compensation."

Such is the plain, unvarnished account of the " affaire Keller," and it is not only absolutely authentic, but beyond all doubt correct in every detail. The Marquise Du Deffand, as is amply proved by her second letter, was scrupulously careful to gather exact information ; she wrote at the very time of the happenings, whilst the other narratives of the scandal, although infinitely more sensational and highly coloured, differ considerably from one another, both in substance and effect.

Jules Janin in the *Revue de Paris*, 1834, describes an orgy with two prostitutes, " a revel of wine and blood " ; Eulenberg uncritically repeats Janin ; the first monograph of Lacroix (1837) merely states that Rosa Keller was indecently flagellated, and the details he added eight years later are trifling and valueless. As we might expect, Restif de la Bretonne in his *Nuits de Paris* (1788) gave full rein to his prolific pen and vivid imagination, and presents us with a nightmare melodrama. Rosa Keller is taken to a mysterious dissecting theatre, where are assembled a number of people, before whom she is to be slowly vivisected. Incidentally she sees the corpses of several former victims, and she utters such piercing shrieks that the assistants retire to make sure there are no servants within hearing. Thereupon she escapes through the window. But enough of such hysterical horrors. The true details of the affair, as Madame Du Deffand relates them, are scandalous and indecent, no doubt, but they are not murderous and ghoulish as later writers would have them be. It was, in fact, an incident which could have been easily paralleled in the Parisian brothels of the day, and is by no means unknown in modern houses of accommodation.

The Marquis, none the less, was confined for a while in the Château of Saumur, whence he was transferred to a prison at Lyons. In six weeks, however, he regained his liberty, and Rosa Keller received an indemnity of 100 louis, with which dowry she soon found a husband. But M. de Montreuil, who had obtained the order for his son-in-law's release, had also procured a special mandate which forbade him to return to Paris, and fixed as his future residence the Château de la Coste, a family possession, situated at no great distance from Marseilles. Here his wife joined him, and she committed the imprudence of also inviting her sister, who had just left the convent and was now a beautiful girl of twenty-one. At the sight of Louise the passion of the Marquis revived, if possible with intenser force than before. But in spite of his avowal that his irregularities were the effect of his disappointed love, she seemed to meet his advances coldly, and in a state bordering on despair he plunged into even wilder excesses than before.

June 21st, 1772, de Sade happened to be in Marseilles on business. He was attended only by his confidential valet, whom he has drawn as Jasmin in *Justine*. That evening he visited a well-known house in the town where he was received with great amiability by the prostitutes who resided there. A sumptuous dinner was presently served at the Marquis's expense, and all drank freely of burgundy and champagne. During the courses he had handed round a box of chocolates of so exquisite a flavour that everyone present partook. The sweets, however, had been subtly treated with cantharides, and the result of the wine and the aphrodisiac was soon apparent. A riotous scene ensued, and for some days after several of the company were exceedingly unwell. Local gossip soon began to paint the incident in very lurid colours, and before long it reached the ears of the Chancellor Maupeon. This good magistrate, who aimed at a great reputation for Draconian severity and was accordingly very jealous for the fair name of the city, particularly hated de Sade, whom he had been watching with an anxious eye. He avidly seized upon this opportunity to make a terrific example of so notorious an offender against morality, and on the 5th of July following laid a plaint before the Parliament of Aix. The Marquis, however, was warned in time. At first he contemplated suicide, and calmly announced this intention to Louise. Thereupon her reserve utterly broke down and she consented to fly with him to Italy. The frontier was immediately crossed, and when the justices arrived in full force at the Château de la Coste to demand their victim he was far beyond their reach. None the less, in an outburst of baffled rage, the Parliament of Aix, presided over by the irate Chancellor, on the 11th of September solemnly declared the Marquis and his valet contumacious and outlaws, and condemned them both to death on a charge of poisoning, to which was superadded an indictment for sodomy, at that time a capital offence.

The accusation of poisoning is manifestly absurd. It is true that Bauchment and Restif de la Bretonne give long and extravagant accounts of the Marseilles orgy, and Bauchment in particular declares that two girls expired from the effects of the drug. But the narratives are as false as they are sensational. Aphrodisiacs and sexual stimulants were in common use among gay society at that time. Binz in his *Pharmacology* (Berlin, 1894) expressly states that quantities of cantharides were employed in France in the mid-eighteenth century. These bonbons or chocolates mixed with satyrion had been introduced into France by the gallants in the train of Catherine de Medici, and a century and a half later the Duc de Richelieu was so well known for his trick of offering such sweets to unsuspecting ladies that his name was actually given to a certain cachou of the kind. Madame Du Barry's " pastilles de sérail " were equally famous.

The actual sentence was not quashed until six years later, June 30th, 1778, when the Marquis was fined fifty francs, a penalty which of itself shows that the savage judgement of the Parliament had been originally engineered by some private rancour and hate.

The few weeks that de Sade passed with Louise in Italy were undoubtedly the happiest of his life. But their union was brief, and she had not attained her twenty-second birthday when, after a sudden illness, she expired in the arms of her lover.[1] His anguish was terrible and he frantically sought oblivion in fresh profligacy. For some reason that is not plain, towards the end of the year he ventured from Geneva to Chambéry, where he was recognized and arrested, and conveyed to the Château de Miolans in Savoy. Hence he escaped in May, 1773, and again took refuge in Italy. He did not return to France until 1777. Upon the 14th of January of that year, however, he was seized at the house of a courtesan at Paris where he had imprudently shown himself, and the same evening he was removed to Vincennes. In June, 1778, he was brought before the Parliament of Aix, but the Advocate Siméon so brilliantly defended his cause that the existing sentence was annulled, and, as we have seen, a trifling fine imposed. Unhappily, owing to the influence of his father-in-law, the decision of this tribunal was over-ridden, and de Sade again became an inmate of Vincennes. In 1784, he was transferred to the Bastille, and on July 13th, 1789, the very eve of the fall of that fortress, to Charenton. In the following year, however,

[1] Another account says that they were forcibly separated, and she was compelled to take the veil. But the above is the most authoritative.

by a decree of the Constitutional Assembly, dated March 29th, he was set at liberty.

Thus from 1777–1790, from the age of thirty-seven to that of fifty, when his exceptional vigour of body and exceptional activity of mind were both at their prime, for thirteen long years, de Sade was kept in closest confinement. Not able to satisfy himself either physically or intellectually his unrefreshed imagination fed upon itself and he became saturnine, melancholy, a dreamer, whose sick dreams were often of the most incredible fantasies and dark eroticism, extravagant and cruel voluptuousness. As Dr. Havelock Ellis has admirably said : " Shut out from real life, he solaced his imagination with the perverted visions—to a very large extent, however, founded on knowledge of the real facts of perverted life in his time—which he has recorded in *Justine*, *Juliette*, and the rest of his many romances." It is infinitely to be regretted that his diaries contained in thirteen large notebooks, which he kept during his imprisonment, have been destroyed. De Sade has been ignorantly paralleled with Gilles de Rais, but Anatole France, in a very striking passage, emphatically rejects such a juxtaposition : " It is monstrously unjust. Gilles de Rais obscenely mutilated his victims in actual practice ; de Sade has described such scenes, which is quite enough indeed, but he never tortured women and children. The indecent flagellation of Rosa Keller and the bonbons with which he regaled the courtesans at Marseilles are no doubt reprehensible exploits, but they are not in the same category as the foul mutilations that Nero is suspected and Gilles de Rais known to have perpetrated. . . . Both the scandal of the ' petite maison ' at Arcueil and that of the supper at Marseilles only became public owing to accidental circumstances, and it is quite certain that de Sade never even attempted murder. The most severe moralist will not place imaginary crimes and those that have actually been committed on the same footing."

We have already noted that Algolagnia, the relation of the sex impulse to pain, is recognized by our greatest living authority as one of the most difficult yet one of the most fundamental problems in the whole range of sexual psychology. It includes two separate groups of feelings which are complementary : " one, in the masculine line, which delights in displaying force and often inflicts pain or the simulacrum of pain ; the other, in the feminine line, which delights in submitting to that force, and even

finds pleasure in a slight amount of pain,[1] or the idea of pain
when associated with the experiences of love." The tendency
of feminine nature to delight in experiencing a certain degree of
physical violence and even actual pain when inflicted by a lover
is certainly normal, but this purely normal manifestation is apt
insensibly to pass over into the region of the morbid. What a
feminine nature seeks to receive a masculine nature is impelled
to give, and hence Garnier is undoubtedly right when he states
that a certain degree of sadism is normal.[2]

The definitions of sadism given by Krafft-Ebing, Moll, Féré,
and other writers differ very considerably, but the detailed and
elaborate definition drawn up by Bloch is strictly based upon
de Sade's works and accordingly, as cited by Havelock Ellis,
Studies in the Psychology of Sex, Vol. III, 1913, p. 106, is the
most pertinent to quote in the present context : " A connexion,
whether intentionally sought or offered by chance, of sexual
excitement and sexual enjoyment with the real or only symbolic
(ideal, illusionary) appearance of frightful and shocking events,
destructive occurrences and practices, which threaten or destroy
the life, health, and property of man and other living creatures,
and threaten and interrupt the continuity of inanimate objects,
whereby the person who from such occurrences obtains sexual
enjoyment may either himself be the direct cause, or cause them
to take place by means of other persons, or merely be the
spectator, or finally, be, voluntarily or involuntarily, the object
against which these processes are directed."

Although de Sade gives his name to this psychological impulse
there have been, of course, from the earliest times many striking
cases of so fundamental an emotion. The examples history offers
us are for the most part of an extravagant and extreme nature, such
as the emperor Tiberius [3]; Caligula, who whilst he caressed the
neck of a wife or a mistress would often cry, " To think it only
needs a word of mine for this charming throat to be slit across ! "
and who threatened Caesonia with torture to compel her to reveal

---

[1] It is probable that something of this masochistic feeling lies (perhaps quite
unconsciously) at the root of the fascination so universally exercised by uncanny
tales of ghosts and spectres, which send hearers or readers to bed shuddering and
glancing over their shoulders with delicious apprehension of a supernatural
visitant.

[2] P. Garnier, *Des Perversions Sexuelles*, Thirteenth International Congress of
Medicine, Section of Psychiatry, Paris, 1900.

[3] *Suetonius*, Tiberius, 44, 61, 62.

why he loved her so madly [1]; Nero; Domitian; Commodus; Caracalla; Heliogabalus,[2] and in fine, the greater number of Rome's Cæsars. Dion Cassius in the abstract of his history preserved to us by Xiphilinus hints darkly that Hadrian sacrificed his favourite Antinous in the performance of some magic rites which were sexual as well as necromantic. This is almost certainly untrue, but the fact remains that superstitious ceremonies of a sadistic nature were common under the later Roman Empire, and Hadrian's acknowledged addiction to sorcery made the accusation at least plausible. Lampridius in his life of Heliogabalus records that he ceremonially slew handsome youths of noble birth whom he had abused, " quum inspiceret exta puerilia," and Eusebius asserts the same of Maxentius. Caracalla is said to have offered similar bloody sacrifices, and in the days of the Italian despots—Ezzelino da Romano, Sigismondo Malatesta, Filippo Maria Visconti, Pier Luigi Farnese—such practices were far from unknown. When Faenza fell in 1501 the two young Manfredi were sent to Rome and imprisoned in Hadrian's Mausoleum, where they were secretly murdered at some midnight sabbat of lust and blood. Concerning Astorre's death, Guiccardini writes : " Astorre, che era minore di diciotto anni e di forma eccellente . . . condotto a Roma, saziata prima (secondo che si disse) la libidine di qualcuno fu occultamente insieme con un suo fratello naturale privato della vita." Nardi [3] plainly asserts that it was Cesare Borgia who violated and murdered the lad. Burckhardt questions whether Sigismondo Malatesta's assault on his own son and Pier Luigi Farnese's rape of the young Bishop of Fano " in pontificalibus " were not largely impelled by some extraordinary superstition. But undoubtedly the most outstanding example of the sadism which intermingles and combines with black magic is Gilles de Rais, who was executed in 1440 upon multiplied and proven charges of the

---

[1] *Suetonius*, Caligula, 33.
[2] Heliogabalus was distinctly masochistic as well as sadistic. *Historiæ Augustæ*. Lampridius, *Heliogabalus*. The same temperament, which is not uncommon, is recorded in the case of a Swiss woman who had poisoned several persons and who confessed to experiencing sexual delight from watching their agonies. Whilst in prison she succeeded in poisoning herself, and even during her death struggle she begged for a mirror that she might obtain voluptuous sensations from observing the contortions of her own countenance. It will be remembered that the Marquise de la Brinvilliers found sexual satisfaction in the agonies of her victims. In *Juliette*, Noirceuil sings several stanzas in honour of la Brinvilliers.
[3] *Storie Fiorentine*, lib. iv, 13.

violation and murder of youths and maidens, the evocation of demons, sacrilege and heresy. This was a case of the most extreme kind and Gilles de Rais was, at the end, maniacal.

Another striking instance is that of Ibrahim ihn Ahmed, Prince of Africa and Sicily (A.D. 875). Upon some prediction of his astrologers he had slain in his presence his whole retinue of pages. At another time, sixty youths who had been selected for his pleasures and of whom he had wearied were burnt by gangs of five in a furnace or suffocated in scalding baths. He was jealous of the perpetuation of mankind and directly a wife or concubine showed signs of pregnancy she was strangled, buried alive, or sawn asunder. He also delighted to explore the entrails of his victims and glutted his eyes on their quivering hearts. Like Heliogabalus and Maxentius he was wont to sacrifice his minions for this purpose. Yet at length he abdicated his throne, donned the garb of a dervish, and preached a Moslem crusade. He died of dysentery before the walls of Cosenza in Italy, whither he had led a rabble of fanatics and devotees.

In the cases of Roman Cæsar, Oriental tyrant, mediæval baron, and Renaissance despot, the most fantastically hideous cruelty could be put into actual practice with little or no difficulty, but it must not be for a moment supposed that de Sade himself would have realized his descriptions even had he had complete opportunity. And it cannot be too strongly emphasized that his ideas have not the slightest symptom or trait of any superstitious theory or obscure belief. Such are entirely alien to his mind and thought. His algolagnia was, so to speak, philosophical and speculative, it was cerebral, as indeed sadism so often is. Had he been a monster of cruelty, under the Revolution with whose leaders politically he was in much sympathy, he would have found ample scope for his proclivities. The contrary is the case. Forgetful of their harsh conduct towards himself, and at great personal risk, he saved his aged father-and-mother-in-law from the guillotine. In consequence of this transaction he was suspected of moderatism, and by order of the " Council of General Safety " imprisoned for a term of six months. He was further attacked in a violent pamphlet by Jacques Dulaure, who accused him of mildness and humanitarian sympathies. De Sade was on principle strongly opposed to capital punishment, and always showed himself a trenchant critic of the vile old penal system. But under the Directory he wholly withdrew from the public arena and devoted himself to literature. He was considerably interested in theatrical affairs, and wrote several dramas, one of which, *Oxtiern ; or the Misfortunes of Profligacy*, was produced with marked success during the first week of November, 1791, at the Comédie Française.

The original sketches and many complete pages of his notorious romances were penned during the languor of his long imprisonment from 1777–1790, when his vivid mind, corroded by the enforced monotony and fretted by the resentful sense of bitter injustice, continually dwelt upon the pleasures of past years, detailing to itself each riot and revel of youth but adding sombre and shocking incidents from the depths of its own disillusionment and despair. Of all the romances the most famous undoubtedly are *Justine* and *Juliette*, two works of considerable length, at first published separately, but afterwards together under the title of *The New Justine, or the Misfortunes of Virtue ; followed by the History of Juliette, her sister, or the Prosperity of Vice*, 1797, 10 volumes, 12mo, the first four of which contain *Justine*, the remaining six *Juliette*. There are an hundred illustrations, some of which are excessively free. *Justine* first appeared in 1791, in which year there were two issues, 8vo and 12mo. In 1792, the second edition was published, and a third followed in 1794. *Juliette* was printed in 1796, 4 vols., 8vo, but the definitive edition of these two romances is that of 1797, as has already been mentioned. It should be noticed that the issues of *Justine* in 1791 differ very widely from those of 1792 and 1794. The latter are far fuller, and, it must be confessed, more naked and more sinister.

It has, I think, escaped the attention of all writers on de Sade that in these amazing and powerful romances we have two very marked examples of the Picaresque School, the novel of deep philosophy and light adventures, whose classic exemplars appear in the great and wondrous work of Petronius and the exotic pages of Apuleius. Extraordinarily popular in Spain, where *Lazarillo de Tormès* is perhaps the best known of an enormous library, it greatly influenced France, and it was here the genius of Le Sage gave the world the modern masterpiece of that style, *Gil Blas*. The Picaresque Romance is so akin to life that it can never die, and its spirit still permeates fiction. A series of more or less disconnected and seemingly inconsequent adventures : domestic, melodramatic ; in town, in country, in court, in village; a panorama of every rank and every profession, king, peasant, capitalist, beggar, vestal, whore; from its very tergiversations and vagaries, now a philosophical discourse that Bacon might have fathered, now a sordid scene as realistic as the photography of Zola, a picaresque romance almost defies analysis unless we are prepared to give a meticulously detailed and indeed paginal account. For this reason, if none other, it is impossible here even to outline the multitudinous incidents that form the history of Justine and Juliette. It must suffice to say that Justine and Juliette are the two daughters of a Parisian banker, who fails, and leaves the penniless orphans to make their own way in the world. Justine, who prizes her chastity like a second Lucrece, unfortunately falls into the hands of a succession of men, who rob her of what she holds most dear, and make her no return. She has adventures with brigands, coiners, monks,[1] magistrates, doctors, nobles, all amid the most fantastic orgies, and the whole while she is persecuted and miserable. Juliette, who sets a price upon her favours and yields to the highest bidder only, commences her career as the mistress of an important Minister of State. She next marries a wealthy count, who has become enamoured of her, and after his death she travels in great state through Italy, residing in Turin, Florence, Rome (where she has an interview with Pius VII), and finally Naples, becoming an important figure at the luxurious Court of Ferdinand and Caroline. In each city she visits the haunts of pleasure, and the erotic is seemingly exhausted in the wealth of description thereby entailed.

Aline et Valcour, published in 1793, 4 vols., 18mo, as by " the Citizen Sade," was written at the Bastille, " one year before the Revolution." This remarkable work is presented in the epistolary form so greatly in vogue during the eighteenth century, and so conspicuously used in England by the sentimental Richardson. De Sade's romance consists of eighty-two letters, some of great

---

[1] De Sade's description of the Benedictine monastery in *Justine* can almost be paralleled in fact. In 1660 the abbey of la Trappe was the resort of the worst characters, male and female, of the countryside. The building was little better than a ruin. Gaillardin terms it " l'habitation des démons " (*Histoire de la Trappe*, I, pp. 46–48). At the abbey of Septfons in the Bourbonnais there were at the beginning of the last century four monks, " coquins," who spent their time in hunting, fishing, coursing and sport. When the abbot, who lived twenty miles off, remonstrated, they attempted to poison him, and he was obliged to pension them. In the eighteenth century in France, monastic life, tainted by the general corruption, was at its lowest ebb.

length, wherein the author allows his characters to formulate his ideas on government, morality, the relation of the sexes, education, political economy, and almost every conceivable subject. It is a powerful and original story, full of interest and not without passion and tenderness. Aline, whom Valcour loves, suffers at the hands of her family because she refuses to wed an old libertine of fortune. There is a long episode, alien to the main theme of the book, which introduces us to the Inquisition of Madrid, but it may be mentioned that the horrors of this Tribunal are very sparingly displayed. Valcour's last letter to his friend, Détérville, when he learns of Aline's death, is infinitely pathetic, the despairing cry of a broken heart.

La Philosophie dans le Boudoir, published in 1795, 2 vols., 16mo, consists of seven dialogues, distinctly pornographic, but not without some clear reasoning in the more didactic passages, which are frequent. De Sade wrote a number of short stories of merit and also left a vast amount of manuscript material from which, in 1904, Iwan Bloch printed *The 120 days of Sodom, or the School of Profligacy*, written at the Bastille in the winter of 1785. Here the author scientifically classifies and catalogues every passion and every aberration ; he calmly investigates and lucidly explains ; and it has been said, " one hundred years before Krafft-Ebing he compiled a complete *Psychopathia Sexualis*." Iwan Bloch gives it is his opinion that it is almost impossible to exaggerate the importance of this work, he even does not hesitate to say that it places de Sade in the front rank of writers of the eighteenth century.

In Messidor, VIII (July, 1800), the Marquis de Sade was unwise enough to publish a political lampoon, *Zoloé . . . A Few Years in the Life of Three Fine Women*. The satire on Josephine, Madame Tallien, Madame Visconti, is very severe, and even the first Consul himself and Barras appear under the thinnest disguise. Moreover the frontispiece of this indiscreet little book represents the three heroines in gauzy Greek attire compelled to unmask before the Genius of History. *Zoloé* was eagerly read on every side, and great scandal ensued. Napoleon, who never forgave, after the first sensation had just a little died down, arbitrarily signed an order for the arrest of de Sade on several quite invalid and impertinent counts, and March 5th, 1801, the Marquis was imprisoned in Sainte-Pélagie. Thence he was transferred to Bicêtre, and, after it had been diligently given out that he was insane, he became, in 1803, an inmate of the asylum at Charenton.

The Marquis de Sade died at ten o'clock in the evening of the December 2nd, 1814. He was seventy-four years old, and for some months his health had been failing, but he had never shown the slightest symptom of insanity or mental decay. In his will, executed January 30th, 1806, he directs that his body shall be buried in the depths of a wood on his own estate, and when the grave is covered, the ground is to be thickly planted with acorns. It has been said that there are few human documents so filled with bitterness and sorrow as this testament. The instructions, however, were not carried out, but an autopsy was performed by three celebrated doctors, who, it is interesting to note, in their report state that the skull was small, remarkably well formed, and could almost have been taken for that of a woman.

The Marquis left two sons: Louis-Marie, born August 27th, 1767 ; Donatien Claude-Armand ; and one daughter, Madeleine-Laure, who died at Echauffour as late as 1844.

There are perhaps few figures around whom ignorance has accumulated more extravagant and impossible legends than it has heaped on the name of the Marquis de Sade. Scion of a decadent and etiolated house, the victim of heredity, environment, political rancour and disappointed love, persecuted and imprisoned for his audacities and misfortunes rather than for the faults he shared with his peers and companions, his abnormal genius at last found vent in the composition of those famous romances wherein by some perverse caprice he has not scrupled to detail his wildest erotic dreams, and has pushed his amazing fancies beyond all bounds of possibility and sound reason. Small wonder perhaps that the man has been entirely confounded with his work, concerning which there is such idle mystery and stupid secrecy. That he has pages of flagrant obscenity no one seeks to deny, but are we to underestimate his importance, nay, to blot out his very name, because of these ? According to de Sade it is only through the sexual that the world can be grasped and understood. Nor can there be a profounder truth ; for the sexual, rightly comprehended, is deep down at the living heart of all humanity, all philosophy, wisdom, and religion.

A RESTORATION PROMPT-BOOK

A RESTORATION PROMPT-BOOK

SOME ninety years ago, whilst William Gifford was engaged upon his Recension of Shirley, the Rev. Robert Watts,[1] Librarian of Sion College, informed him that they there possessed a copy of *The Sisters* which contained no inconsiderable number of manuscript notes in an early hand. Gifford, who seems to have examined these with some care but little perception, writes in his introduction to that comedy (Shirley's *Works*, V, p. 354) :—

> It turned out to be merely the prompter's copy. The book appears to have belonged to Davenant's company, in Drury Lane, and must, from the names, have been in use about 1666. It is piteously scrawled; and there are characters dispersed along the margin, *interiore nota*, and such as the initiated alone probably understand.

He then proceeds to give the names of the performers " collected from the margin," and concludes, " I am unable to appropriate the names to the characters—for they appear in the margin long before they enter, and are set down as hints to the prompter to urge them to make ready." Gifford's list of actors is, it may be observed, very faulty and incomplete. Dyce, who materially supervised Gifford's work and saw this edition of Shirley through the press in 1833, had nothing, however, to add to these remarks, and thenceforward the Sion College copy of *The Sisters* has been totally forgotten and ignored. Even Nason's study of Shirley (1915), a book of copious, if somewhat yeasty, detail, has no mention of this particular copy, and Forsythe, in his *Shirley's Plays and the Elizabethan Drama* (1914), was so misled by Gifford's confused and superficial account that, although dealing with *The Sisters* at considerable length, he has nothing more than a casual reference to a " M.S. of the play at Sion College," whence

---

[1] This eminent scholar and bibliophile was born *circa* 1750. April 26th, 1799, he was appointed Chief Librarian of Sion College, where he had been Assistant Librarian since 1785. In the summer of 1799 he was inducted by Bishop Porteous to the rectorship of St. Alphege. He died January 19th, 1842.

he quotes an additional couplet, assigned on Gifford's authority to Davenant.

The copy in question, however, is not a manuscript, but the octavo volume, " Six New Playes, viz. : *The Brothers, Sisters, Doubtful Heir, Imposture, Cardinall, Court Secret.* . . . All written by James Shirley. Never printed before. London. Printed for Humphrey Robinson at the Three Pigeons, and Humphrey Moseley at the Prince's Armes in St. Paul's Church-yard, 1653." [1] Upon examining the Sion College copy of *The Sisters* I at once became aware that we have here something of unique interest and value, the importance of which had entirely escaped both Gifford and Dyce, neither of whom, truth to tell, was adequately acquainted with the more intimate stage conditions of the Elizabethan and Restoration theatres.

The Sion College copy of *The Sisters* is indeed, as Gifford saw, " the prompter's copy." It did not, however, belong to Davenant's company in Drury Lane, as he blunderingly states. The actors' names are those of Killigrew's company, which then occupied the Theatre Royal in Bridges Street, Covent Garden. [2] The home of Davenant's company from June, 1661, to the autumn of 1671 was the first Duke's Theatre in Lincoln's Inn Fields. Hence the assignment to Davenant of interpolated rhyming tags which are marginally scribbled to round off Acts II and V of *The Sisters* is manifestly absurd. Again, as will be shown later when a date is suggested, the book cannot have been in use as early as 1666. I have no doubt that the manuscript notes and marginalia are in the hand of Charles Booth, who was, as Downes tells us, " sometime Book-Keeper " at the Theatre Royal. Here, then, we have the only prompt-book of the Restoration theatre that has come down to us, and this is a fact of very special importance, as, although there are in existence several manuscript prompt-books of earlier days, this is the only copy of a prompt-book belonging to the nascent Picture Stage, the era when scenery and changes of scene had just come into general and public use.

Moreover we are able to add another important rôle to the list of characters played by Nell Gwyn. Save for this prompt

---

[1] Each play has a separate title-page. The first five bear date 1652, but the last, *The Court Secret*, in agreement with the joint title-page to the volume, has 1653.

[2] The term " Drury Lane " as applied to a theatre dates from about 1690 (see W. J. Lawrence, *The Elizabethan Playhouse*, Second Series, pp. 76, 77).

book, too, there is no record at all, neither in Pepys, nor in Downes, nor in any other contemporary, of a revival of *The Sisters* after the Restoration.

Gifford declared that he was unable " to appropriate the names to the characters," but none the less the various actors' names are so systematically jotted down some twenty or more lines before the several entrances throughout the play of the character each performer sustained that, with a little care, we can exactly assign the rôles as follows :—

Prince Farnese	Beeston
Contarini	[William] Harris
Antonio	[William] Cartwright
Frapolo	Dick Bell
Longino	Graydon
Rangino	Reeves
Lucio	[Marmaduke] Watson
Giovanni	Lydall
Stephanio	Littlewood
Piperollo	Joe Haines
Scholar.	Littlewood
Paulina	Mrs. Knepp
Angellina	Mrs. Hughes
Pulcheria [Vergerio]	Nell Gwyn
Francescina	Mrs. Yokney

From the above cast the date of the revival of *The Sisters* can be narrowed down to one possible period. It must have taken place between 1668 and 1671. Joe Haines was at the Nursery, in Hatton Garden, *circa* 1667, and only joined the Theatre Royal Company in February or March, 1668. Nell Gwyn retired from the stage not later than 1671, and Dick Bell lost his life in the Drury Lane fire of January, 1672, as is recorded in a *Newsletter*, dated January 27th, 1671[2] :—

A fire at the King's Playhouse between 7 and 8 oclock on Thursday evening last, which half burned down the house and all their scenes and wardrobe ; and all the houses from the Rose Tavern in Russell Street on that side of the way of Drury Lane are burned and blown up with many in Vinegar Yard ; 20,000l. damage. The fire began under the stairs where Orange Moll keeps her fruit. Bell the player was blown up.

According to Downes, Bell, Reeves, and Harris, " were bred up from boys under the Master Actors."

Nell Gwyn was probably cast for a " breeches part," Pulcheria, who masquerades in male attire as Vergerio, page to Contarini, owing to her great success as Florimel, in Dryden's *Secret Love*,[1] produced in February, 1667. Florimel, it will be remembered, to turn the tables on a wayward suitor, comes in like a young gallant, " a very janty fellow, *poudré et ajusté*, as well as the best of 'em." Vergerio, however, is a sentimental character, something resembling Beaumont and Fletcher's Bellario, the disguised Euphrasia, a rôle which, in 1668, Nell Gwyn played to the Philaster of Charles Hart.

It is interesting to note that the old prompter always jots down in his margin, " Mrs Ellen " or " Mrs Nelle," never " Mrs Gwyn."

My references to the text of *The Sisters* are to the Gifford-Dyce recension, Vol. V, pp. 353–424, as being the most easily accessible edition of the play. In the prompt-book, at Act I, Scene 1, we have the marginal note " A wood stands," and at Frapolo's line " That shall become our trade and constitutions " (p. 361, l. 20), is written " noise ready " for the " A noise within," twenty-one lines later. At Piperollo's " I will conduct you " (p. 363, l. 31), in the margin is written " Mr Lydall Mr Littlewood," and at Frapolo's " The devil wore in the last anti-masque," " Mr Cartrite Mrs Hughes," indications of the subsequent entrances of Giovanni and Stephanio, and, a little after, of Antonio and Angellina, who pass over the stage. At the entry of Giovanni and Stephanio (p. 365) is noted " ⊙ Castle." The mark ⊙ undoubtedly indicates a change of scene, and Mr. W. J. Lawrence, in a letter to myself, suggests that it means " Whistle for change." It must be remembered that in the Restoration Theatre the curtain normally rose at the beginning and fell at the end of the play. The termination of an act was shown by a clear stage.[2] At Stephanio's line " Though he were a gallant man " (p. 365, l. 3), " Mrs Nep " is written in the margin for Paullina's entrance twenty-seven lines after. At Lucio's " The Lord Contarini is arriv'd at the castle " (p. 368, l. 22), there is a manuscript note, " Act Ready." This occurs eighteen lines before the end of the act, and at the last line the prompter has written " Ring." " Act Ready " must refer to the preliminary warning of the musicians

---

[1] See Pepys, March 2nd, March 25th, May 24th, 1667, etc.
[2] See W. J. Lawrence, *The Elizabethan Playhouse*, First Series, pp. 170–177, where are given detailed particulars of this convention.

for the inter-act music, and may be paralleled with the Elizabethan
" Whilst the Act plays," as in Marston's *Parasitaster*, Act V, to
which is prefixed the stage-direction " Whilst the Act is a-playing,
Hercules and Tiberio enter. . . ." The direction " Ring " is
undoubtedly the signal for the musicians to commence. Curiously
enough, it has crept into one printed play. The conclusion of
the first act of Sedley's *The Mulberry Garden*, produced at the
Theatre Royal, Monday, May 18, 1668 (4to, 1668), stands thus :—

> *Alth.* Farewel, *Diana*, and be sure you do
>   Nothing unworthy of your Love and Vow.
> *Ring.*
>   *Exeunt* Diana *and* Althea *severally.*

At Act II, Scene 1, of *The Sisters* (p. 369) the prompter's notes
are " Haines 3 bags. ⊙ fabies house & landskape." Three or
four lines after the act has begun, Piperollo, who has robbed his
parents, rushes in masked and clutching three bags of money.
At Piperollo's line, " These things must be employ'd to better
uses " (p. 370, l. 19) we have " Mr Watson Mr Lydall Mr
Littlewood wth staffes," and for the change of scene " ⊙
Presence." Scene 2 opens with the stage direction " Enter
Lucio, Giovanni, and Stephanio with white staves." At
Giovanni's line, " Twill be sport " (p. 372, l. 9) is written
" Mrs. Ellen, Mr. Cartrite, Mr. Harris." Contarini, Antonio,
Vergerio duly enter twenty-four lines later. A little before this
at Giovanni's " as all the royal blood, Had muster'd in his
girles
veins " there is noted " Mrs Nep 2 women " ; and twenty-six
lines before Paulina's entrance " Florish ready." Here and there
throughout the scene the prompter has struck through a superfluous line or two, but the omissions are brief and trifling.
Twenty-nine lines before the end of the act, at Antonio's " If
thou canst speak any " (p. 379, l. 15) we find " Act Ready "
marked. At the end of Act II is written in the couplet :

u
For though I am no Princess yo shall see
such state that Princess born shall learn of me,

which Gifford so carelessly ascribed to Davenant.

Act III, Scene 1 (p. 380), has the note " A Roome in ye ⊙
castle," and at Giovanni's " starch-faced Egyptians " (p. 381,

l. 14) the prompter has " all yᵉ Banditi " for the entrance some
dozen speeches later of the disguised thieves. In this acting
version the Song " Beauty, and the various graces " is marked
for omission. Towards the end of this first scene at the Country-
man's speech " Know our Princess ? " (p. 388, l. 22) the prompter
has " Mrs Nelle Antonio Contarini " for the entrance of Antonio,
Contarini, and Vergerio. He also marks the new scene which
obviously commences at this point ⊙. Probably a pair of
conventionally interior flats were drawn over. " Ring " is
marked at the cue " vestal name " (p. 392, l. 16), Francescina's
last three lines being cut.

The beginning of Act IV is marked " ⊙ wood." The flats
would here have been opened. At Strozzo's line " What's the
mystery ? " (p. 396, l. 23) we have " Mrs Hughes Mrs Yokney "
for the subsequent entrance of Angellina and Francescina, at
which point the prompter writes " Angellina's Chamber ⊙."
At Francescina's line, " The gentlewomen were commended,
madam " (p. 397, l. 24), is marginally marked " Littlewood,"
whose name is repeated four lines later. This double entry was
no doubt made to remind the prompter that the actor must be
warned to be ready in his changed costume. Littlewood was
doubling the rôles of Stephanio and the Scholar. The third,
fourth, and fifth scenes of Act IV are noted " ⊙ Court or
Chamber," " ⊙ Chamber," " ⊙ Court or Castle." In the last
scene, at Farnese's " When a clear eye is judge " (p. 408, l. 20),
the prompter has written " Every body be ready " in preparation
for the grand entrance of Frapolo, Paulina, and their train
thirty-eight lines later. " Flourish ready " is noted at Contarini's
" I rate no expectation " (p. 408, l. 24), and " Flourish here "
three lines before Bell, Mrs. Knepp, and the rest actually appeared
on the stage. " Act ready " is marked at Farnese's " What
gentleman is that ? " twenty-three lines before the conclusion,
and " Ring " at the last couplet of the scene.

In Act V the first scene is marked " ⊙ A Chamber," the
second and last scene " ⊙ Court." Amongst other notes we
have in Scene 2, at Lucio's " When did your lordship see his
highness ? " (p. 417, l. 18) " Mr Beeston Mrs Hughes Ellen &
                                                              ts
attendants." Farnese, Vergerio, Angellina, and a train enter
some dozen speeches later. At Paulina's speech " It is my
wonder, . . ." (p. 419, l. 14) the prompter notes " Dicke all

the Banditts " for the entrance of Frapolo and the banditti
fifteen lines after. Frapolo is given a tag to end the play.

> *Bell.* Tho my State's gone some rule I will yet have
> for her I married I will make my slave.

In giving this account of the only known Restoration prompt-
book I have been obliged to pass over many notes and marginalia
which could only be intelligible if the Sion College copy of *The
Sisters* were reproduced in facsimile. But I venture to think
I have detailed fair specimens of all the prompter's scribblings
which are of value, I do not say of interest.

It is curious that *The Sisters* should be the only play in the
volume which has been thus annotated and used by Booth,
for of the other dramas therein contained we know that *The
Court Secret*, " prepared for the scene at the Black-Friers," but
unacted before the Restoration, was produced as " a new play "
on August 18th, 1664, and frequently revived in the ensuing
decade. Between November, 1660, and July, 1662, there are
recorded several performances of *The Brothers*. *The Cardinal*,
in particular, was one of the Stock tragedies of Killigrew's
company. It was seen by Pepys at the Cockpit as early as
October 2nd, 1662 ; at the Theatre Royal, with Charles Hart and
Becke Marshall in the cast, on August 24th, 1667 ; and again at
the Theatre Royal, April 27th, 1668. With regard to this last
tragedy, indeed, the prompter has in the Sion College copy
scored through with his pen the dialogue of fifteen lines in
Act I, Scene 2, between Valeria and Celinda from " Is not the
general a gallant man ? " to " Thou art wild ; we may be
observ'd." He also marks for omission Celinda's line, " He
has been taught to kiss," which occurs a little earlier in the same
scene. But there are no further notes or manuscript directions
of any kind, and consequently this copy could not have been
that in use at the theatre.

Upon an examination of this Restoration prompt-book of
The Sisters, the first thing that strikes us is the extreme paucity of
prompter's directions. Beyond an indication of the various
changes of scene, a note of some special property to be carried
or used by an actor, and the actors' names to be called for their
cues, there are hardly any further directions of any kind.

Of the actors in *The Sisters* Cartwright and Haines are famous
names. Dick Bell, Watson, Lydall were performers of con-

siderable importance at the time. Reeve was perhaps the
brother of Dryden's mistress, the actress Ann Reeve. Beeston
must not be confounded with William Beeston, the manager ;
nor William Harris of the King's House with Henry Harris,
Davenant's " star." Nell Gwyn had as yet but newly attracted
the King's attention ; Mrs. Hughes was soon to draw Prince
Rupert from his laboratory ; Mrs. Knepp we know from the
pages of Pepys. Mrs. Yokney's name I have never found in
any other printed cast of Restoration actors, but she appears in a
list of Theatre Royal actresses to whom " liveries " were to be
given by a Lord Chamberlain's warrant, October 2, 1669. It is
interesting to note that with the exception of Graydon, Reeves,
Joe Haines,[1] and Mrs. Yokney, all the actors and actresses who
appeared in this revival of *The Sisters* are among the printed casts
of Dryden's *Evening's Love* (1668), *Tyrannick Love* (1669), and *The
Conquest of Granada* (1670–1).

[1] It has been erroneously stated that his first rôle on the public stage was Benito
in Dryden's *The Assignation* (1672).

MRS. COREY:
PEPYS' "DOLL COMMON"

MRS. COREY: PEPYS' "DOLL COMMON"

MRS. COREY [1] (or Cory), who was one of the earliest of our English actresses, probably made her appearance on the boards in December, 1660. Her name indeed stands first in Downes' list of Killigrew's ladies, but perhaps it would be perilous to draw any particular inference from this. On or about November 8th, 1660, the King's players had removed from the old Red Bull in St. John Street, Clerkenwell, an un-roofed house built as early as 1600, where they had been acting for some three or four months, to a new theatre situated in Bear Yard, Vere Street, Clare Market. This, an oblong roofed house, built in a tennis-court, was the last theatre to be constructed upon the Elizabethan model. It was here that professional actresses first regularly appeared. [2] Although it is often claimed that Margaret Hughes, Prince Rupert's mistress, was the first English actress, this should not be positively asserted. It is highly probable that Thomas Jordan's " *A Prologue to introduce the first Woman that came to Act on the Stage in the Tragedy call'd* The Moor of Venice " was spoken at Vere Street on December 8th, 1660, when *Othello* was played there, and that Mrs. Hughes was the Desdemona on that occasion. But beyond this it is impossible to speak with certainty. The first time that Pepys saw women on the stage was in the sylvan and sunshiny *Beggar's Bush*, Thursday, January 3rd, 1661. The next day however he saw *The Scornful Lady* with the title-rôle acted by a man. Three days later he takes his wife to *The Silent Woman*. Ned Kynaston, a lad of twenty, played Epicoene, and Mrs. Corey the boisterous breeches-wearing Mistress Otter. [3] " Among other things here, Kinaston,

---

[1] The name is also spelled Corye, Coey, and in a MS. Core.
[2] This is strictly true as a generalization, which is hardly affected by such an exception as that when Mrs. Coleman was the Ianthe in Davenant's opera *The Siege of Rhodes*.
[3] The casts of these early revivals are generally from Downes. It should perhaps be remarked that the rôle of Epicoene must be played by a young actor. If it be assigned to a woman the *dénouement* is meaningless. Yet it seems to have been

the boy, had the good turn to appear in three shapes : first as a
poor woman in ordinary clothes to please Morose ; then in fine
clothes, as a gallant ; and in them was clearly the prettiest woman
in the whole house ; and lastly, as a man ; and then likewise did
appear the handsomest man in the house." The fair and frail
dames of the court were wholly of the diarist's opinion, and many
a time would duchess or countess take the pretty boy, just as
he left the stage in woman's skirts, and hale him away into her
coach for a turn in Hyde Park or to eat a sillabub at the Mulberry-
Garden, proud to flaunt her prize before the gaze of the fashionable crowd. It was indeed a favourite prank of both actors and
actresses to walk the streets in their gaudy stage costumes. One
evening Harry Harris, of the Duke's Theatre, and la belle Pierce
brought to Pepys' house a country wench, seemingly just come
up to London, demure and shy in her blue stockings and straw
hat, who, to the worthy Samuel's delight, soon proved to be
that " merry jade " Knepp, coming off the stage just as she had
danced and acted the same afternoon in a revival of Suckling's
fantastic yet strangely fascinating extravaganza *The Goblins*.
We must remember that in Restoration days Prince Hal or
Cassio dressed in clothes such as might have been worn in the
Mall an hour before the play began without attracting attention
or remark save perchance by their richness and elegance. In
fact so fond were the young actors of parading their new
suits in public that on April 19th, 1678, an edict was issued
forbidding the players to go outside the theatre in their stage
costumes.

From the very outset Mrs. Corey attained a high reputation,
and in her own line, " old women," she was simply unapproach-
able, far excelling Mrs. Norris, who did the same business at the
rival theatre. On Tuesday, February 12th, 1661, Pepys was at
The Scornful Lady, in which delightful comedy Abigail, the
lickerish waiting-woman with a colt's tooth for men's flesh,
proved one of Mrs. Corey's finest rôles. Mrs. Marshall acted the
Lady, and Knepp the rich Widow, who marries the scapegrace
young Loveless. Five years later (Thursday, December 27th, 1666),

sustained by Mrs. Oldfield and other actresses. When the piece was revived at
Drury Lane, 13 January, 1776, Mrs. Siddons was actually cast for the title-rôle, which
she played thrice. Garrick and Colman then realized their incomprehensible mistake,
and Epicoene was hastily given to Lamash, a handsome young fellow, the original
Trip in *The School for Scandal*. But the mischief had been done, and the revival
was a failure.

the diarist at the King's House again " saw ' The Scornfull Lady ' well acted ; Doll Common doing Abigail most excellently, and Knipp the Widow very well." The name Doll Common is given Mrs. Corey by Pepys owing to her superlative performance of that character in *The Alchemist*, which he saw as early as Saturday, June 22nd, 1661, and rightly judged " an incomparable play." On Thursday, March 14th of the same year, he applauded *A King and No King*. Mrs. Corey acted Arane, the Queen-Mother. Who was the Panthea on this occasion we do not know, but in 1670 Nell Gwyn sustained the Princess, which, being " a great and serious part," she probably did " most basely." In a subsequent revival the rôle fell to Mrs. Betty Cox. On Thursday, March 28th, 1661, Pepys saw that fine tragedy *The Bloody Brother*. It was magnificently cast with Hart as Rollo ; Kynaston, Otto ; Mrs. Marshall, the avenging Edith ; and Mrs. Corey, Sophia, the old Duchess of Normandy.

On Saturday, April 27th, 1661, Pepys was at *The Chances*. He sees the same piece again on Wednesday, October 9th, that year. On both occasions, however, he merely records a visit to the theatre and makes no comment on the play. But it is most noticeable that on Tuesday, February 5th, 1667, when he again sees *The Chances* he is filled with admiration and writes : " A good play I find it, and the actors good in it ; and pretty to hear Knipp sing in the play very properly ' All night I weepe ' ; and sang it admirably. The whole play pleases me well." It is, I think, fairly evident that the play twice seen by Pepys in 1661 was Fletcher's original comedy ; and the play produced in February, 1667,[1] the Duke of Buckingham's excellent alteration wherein the two last acts are wittily re-written and practically new. In the first place the diarist's two visits to *The Chances* in 1661 make no impression on him. In 1667 he is enthusiastic. Dyce in editing *The Chances* says : " In 1682 an alteration or this comedy by the celebrated Villiers, Duke of Buckingham, was brought out at the theatre in Dorset Gardens." This blunder is perhaps due to the fact that Buckingham's *The Chances* was printed quarto, 1682. Sir E. K. Chambers in his recension of the Fletcher comedy (*Beaumont and Fletcher*, Variorum Edition, Vol. IV, 1912) mistakenly follows Dyce without comment. But it can be amply proved that Buckingham's version must

---

[1] Dryden in 1672 speaks of the improvement of the last two acts of *The Chances* as though the alteration were fairly recent, of some half a dozen years date.

have been acted before 1671. The Epilogue has the following couplet :

> Some of the fellows, who have writ before,
> When *Nell* has danc'd her jig, steal to the door,

an allusion to the dancing of Nell Gwyn, an immense attraction at the King's House.[1] Nell Gwyn had retired from the stage in 1671, and such a reference eleven years after must be banal. The whole point is topical, and in 1667 it would have been most pertinent. Nor can it be argued that the Epilogue is an old one dished up for Buckingham's alteration. The opening lines in particular, and the tenor of the whole, exclude that possibility. It commences

> Perhaps you gentlemen expect to-day
> The author of this fag-end of a play—

It was exactly the fag-end which was Buckingham's, the new fourth and fifth acts.

Incidentally it may be remarked that it is certain both Prologues and Epilogues were repeated time after time with little or no alteration far oftener than is generally allowed. A striking example is the Prologue to the revival of Fletcher's splendid tragedy *The Double Marriage* at the King's House in 1671. (The probable cast was Virolet, Hart ; Duke of Sesse, Mohun ; Ascanio, Kynaston ; Juliana, Mrs. Boutel ; Martia, Mrs. Marshall.) This identical Prologue was printed before Mrs. Behn's *Abdelazer*, 4to, 1693, which when it was first issued, 4to, 1677, was published without a Prologue. It also appears as the Epilogue to the same lady's posthumous *The Widdow Ranter*, 4to, 1690. On the last occasion there was one slight change. The allusion to the obsolescent card game Beasts, " Damn'd Beasts and Ombre," became the fashionable Basset, " Basset and Ombre." From the *Stationers' Register* we know that Dryden actually wrote a Prologue and an Epilogue to *The Widdow Ranter*, but curiously enough neither of these can be traced.

In the production of Buckingham's *The Chances*, February, 1667, Hart was the Don John, a part in which he was especially

---

[1] Moll Davis, of the Duke's House, was, it will be remembered, also famous for dancing jigs. On 31 May, 1668, Pepys hears that " At the play at Court the other night Mrs. Davis was there ; and when she was to come to dance her jig, the Queen would not stay to see it."

famous, and which no actor after him, not even Garrick, has ever been able to attempt with the same verve and spirit. Mrs. Corey probably acted the Bawd. After the union of the two companies, this part was also assumed by Mrs. Elinor Leigh, who infused a good deal of humour into " the modish mother . . . affecting to be politely commode for her own daughter." In these later revials the Second Constantia was played by the alluring Charlotte Butler, in which rôle, with all deference to " Mrs. Oldfield's lively performance of the same character," Cibber says she was never excelled. Among the most stupid pieces of criticism ever penned is that of Richard Cumberland, Sheridan's Sir Fretful, in his reviewing *The Chances*. Noting that the last two acts (which, as we have pointed out, entirely belong to Buckingham) are in prose, and that the former three are light and easy verse, Cumberland gravely assigns the verse to Fletcher and the prose to Beaumont !

The fact that Buckingham's version was not printed until 1682, which has misled Dyce into postdating the production fifteen years, points to an important revival, but has no bearing on the date of the original performance. A parallel case is Rochester's *Valentinian*, 4to, 1685, produced in the autumn of 1684 with much advertisement and circumstance. But a version of Rochester's play under the title *Lucina's Rape, or The Tragedy of Vallentinian*, had been put on at the Theatre Royal in 1678, or at the latest in the spring of 1679. Valentinian was acted by Hart ; Aecius, the bluff loyal general, Mohun ; Maximus, William Wintershal ; Pontius, Lydal ; Chylax, Cartwright, tall of stature and resonant of voice ; Lycias, Clarke, young and handsome ; Lucina, Mrs. Marshall ; Claudia, Betty Cox ; Marcellina, " chestnut-maned " Mrs. Boutel ; Ardelia, Mrs. Corey ; Phorba, Mrs. Knepp. The veteran Wintershal, who had been a member of Queen Henrietta Maria's company and acted at the Salisbury Court Theatre in Fleet Street, died in July, 1679. In 1684 Aecius was played by Betterton ; and Lucina by Mrs. Barry ; Cardonell Goodman was the Emperor ; Kynaston, Maximus ; and Philip Griffin, Pontius.

On May 5th, 1662, *The Knight of the Burning Pestle* was revived at the Vere Street Theatre. The cast has not been preserved, but Mrs. Corey probably acted the Citizen's Wife and Kynaston Ralph. The same year we find her as Mrs. Whitebroth in Wilson's *The Cheats*, a capital comedy which, owing to its mordant satire on Nonconformist ministers in the person of Scruple, a Restoration Shepherd Stiggins, created by Lacy, the Puritan party had interest enough temporarily to suppress, but which was soon allowed again. Such indeed are its wit and humour that it kept the boards with triumphant success for well over half-a-century. As late as December, 1727, Hippisley at Lincoln's Inn Fields was playing Scruple to the Mrs. Whitebroth of Mrs. Giffard, when the comedy was followed by *Harlequin Anna Bullen.* At first, however, Scruple with his deep potations, "too good for the wicked : it may strengthen them in their enormities," proved over-broad, and in a letter to John Brooke, dated March 28th, 1663, Abraham Hill writes : " The new play called *The Choats* has been attempted on the stage, but it is so scandalous that it is forbidden." Killigrew however took the script and read a page or two to the King himself. " Oddsfish ! " cried Charles, with a hearty burst of laughter, " play it, man, play it." So were the difficulties overcome. Lacy was so much admired in his part that Michael Wright by royal command painted him on one canvas in three rôles : " *viz.* that of *Teague* in the *Committee*, Mr. *Scruple* in *The Cheats*, and M. *Galliard* in *The Variety*." [1] The picture is now at Hampton Court. The costume, make-up, and facial expression of Parson Scruple are extraordinarily effective.

The Committee, a somewhat similar play to *The Cheats*, scarifying the Parliamentarians with equal zeal, is the best thing from Sir Robert Howard's pen. " Merry but indifferent " is the verdict of Pepys. This comedy also was produced in 1662, and Mrs. Corey doubtless created Mrs. Gillian Day, whilom the errant kitchenmaid, but now " Your Honour " and " Your Ladyship," " with a tongue that wags as much faster than all other women's, as in the several motions of a watch, the hand of the minute moves faster than that of the hour." In spite of the extremely topical politics, *The Committee* had a long lease of life, ample proof of its sterling humour, and was acted at Drury Lane as late as 1788, with Mrs. Hopkins as Mrs. Day ; old Day, Robert Baddeley, of Twelfth-Night-cake fame ; and Moody, Suett, Miss Pope, Miss Kemble in the cast. Shorn of its political satire and curtailed, *The Committee* was put on at Covent Garden, May 9th, 1797, as *The Honest Thieves*, a farce in two acts. Mrs. Davenport was Mrs. Day, and she was well supported by Munden and Macready *père*. *The Honest Thieves* was still played in the third quarter of the nineteenth

---

[1] By the Duke of Newcastle.

century, but, as inevitable, this tinkering at the old comedy has spoiled Howard's scenes not a little.

On Thursday, May 7th, 1663, Killigrew opened his new theatre, Drury Lane, as it may be for convenience called, (The Theatre Royal, Bridges Street). Here the company firſt used regular scenery. Vere Street was a platform quasi-Elizabethan ſtage from firſt to laſt, a faſt it may be well to emphasize. In Auguſt, 1664, Pepys saw *The Alchemiſt* [1] at Drury Lane. As we have noted above, it was on account of Mrs. Corey's wonderful presentation of the punk Doll Common in this comedy that he dubs her by that name. The play was incomparably caſt. Mohun aſted the sharking Face, the rogue of a hundred shifts ; Cartwright, Sir Epicure the magnificent, with his dreams of golden wealth greater than Peruvian mines, gems and jewels, " emeralds, saphyres, hiacynths, and rubies," commoner than duſt, banquets of " dissolv'd pearle," and more than mortal delights ; Burt, the suspicious, misbelieving Surly, who, for all his acumen, is finally gulled like the reſt ; Bateman, Tribulation Wholesome, the Puritan paſtor ſtanding up for " the beauteous discipline againſt the rag of Rome " ; Lacy, " hot Ananias," the Anabaptiſt deacon from Amſterdam denouncing " heathen Greek," bells, traditions, Spanish slops, the superſtitious word Chriſtmas— " Chriſt-tide, I pray you " ; Mrs. Rutter, Dame Pliant, the siſter to Kaſtril, the angry boy. Yet there was one unfortunate gap. Walter Clun, the beſt representative of Subtle ever seen on the ſtage, had been murdered on Wednesday, August 3rd, 1664,[2] by highwaymen. After leaving the theatre, Clun had spent a jovial evening, and as he was returning home late to his country house, at Kentish Town, he was set on by padders near Tatnam Court, wounded, bound hand and foot, and flung into a wayside ditch. Here, ſtruggling to release himself, he bled to death. Subtle fell to William Wintershal, but the public never found any aſtor to equal their old favourite. Five years after Pepys writes sadly of *The Alchemiſt,* " It is ſtill a good play, . . . but I do miss Clun for the Doſtor."

On Tuesday, Oſtober 4th, 1663, the diariſt heard a bit of theatrical gossip such as his heart loved. " To-morrow they told us should be aſted, or the day after, a new play called ' The Par-

---

[1] He had previously seen this maſterpiece of Jonson's as early as 1661.
[2] *An Egley Upon The Moſt Execrable Murther of Mr. Clun* says Tuesday night, 2 Auguſt.

son's Dreame ' (*i.e.* Tom Killigrew's *The Parson's Wedding*) acted all by women." A week later Luellin, dining with Pepys, gives him a racy account of the new production. It is indeed a very amusing if lengthy play. It was doubtless originally intended for the Phoenix, or Cockpit as the theatre was termed from having been built in the Cockpit in Drury Lane, and curiously enough the old stage directions of the non-scenic theatre are retained. Mrs. Corey was certainly in the cast, but it would perhaps be too temerarious to hazard a suggestion which part she filled. On Saturday, January 14th, 1665, Pepys saw *Volpone*. Mrs. Corey played Fine Madam Would-be to the Sir Politick of Lacy. The evil old magnifico was Mohun ; Hart, Mosca his scheming para-site ; Cartwright, Corbaccio, doting with age and avarice ; Kynaston, Peregrine, the boyish traveller, doing the grand tour ; Mrs. Marshall, Celia, chaste and lovely ; Shatterel and Burt, Corvino and Voltore, the merchant and the advocate, agog for dead men's shoes.

On Monday, June 5th, 1665, an edict from the Lord Chamber-lain's office stopped all theatrical performances on account of the Plague. This remained in force for about a year and a half, for it was the last week in November, 1666, before the public theatres were permitted to reopen, and even then gossip said that people were still dying of the pestilence and that the Thanksgiving Day for the cessation of the pest (November 20th) had been unduly hurried on merely to allow plays to begin once more with some semblance of decency, since the Bishops absolutely prohibited acting until all danger might be said practically to have come to an end. Even on Friday, December 7th, when Pepys visited the King's Theatre to admire Anne Marshall in *The Maid's Tragedy*, he sat with his cloak shrouding his face, " in mighty pain lest I should be seen by anybody to be at a play." In January, however, matters improved. On Tuesday, January 1st, 1666–67, Killigrew's company revived *The Custom of the Country* with Mrs. Knepp as Guiomar. Mrs. Corey probably played Sulpitia. This was the play Dryden thought the most obscene of any in the whole Reper-tory of Restoration drama, for in the preface to his *Fables*, 1700, he wrote : " There is more Baudry in one Play of *Fletcher's*, called *The Custom of the Country*, than in all ours together. Yet this has been often acted on the Stage in my remembrance." In February Dryden's excellent comedy *Secret Love, or The Maiden Queen*, was produced with an all-star cast. Mrs. Corey created Melissa, the worldly-wise old mother, a part she played with most notable success. This rôle, although quite small, gives opportunity in two richly comic scenes, which however are so brief that the applause she gained is weighty evidence of her outstanding merit. On Wednesday, September 25th, 1667, Pepys saw *The Sea Voyage*, in which Mrs. Corey was probably Rosellia, the part she took eighteen years later in D'Urfey's meddlesome adaptation of Fletcher's romantic drama. On Saturday, October 19th of the same year, was the first performance of Orrery's grandiose heroics *The Black Prince*, in which Mrs. Corey created Lord Dela-were's sister, Cleorin. On Friday, July 31st, 1668, before the King and court, " Mighty Merry," was given, " now new acted," Lacy's farcical *The Old Troop*, in which Mrs. Corey probably acted Dol Troop. On Friday, December 18th, 1668, there was a sumptuous and long-delayed revival of Jonson's *Catiline*, with Hart in the title-rôle ; Mohun, Cethegus, a character he made peculiarly his own ; Burt, Cicero ; and Mrs. Corey, Sempronia. Kynaston, Beeston, Wintershal, Cartwright, Reeves, Thomas Gradwell, and Dick Bell were also in the cast. In this production, which had been urged on Killigrew by Buckingham and Dorset, two ardent Jonsonians, the King himself was interested, and gave the theatre no less a sum than five hundred pounds for costumes. The town talked long and loudly of the number of men-hirelings (as supers were picturesquely called) ; of the sixteen scarlet robes to be worn in the Senate scene, which was particularly fine and magni-fical ; of the battle entailing all the resources of the stage. As a *bonne bouche* this ultra-classical tragedy was ushered in with a Pro-logue " merrily spoken by Mrs. *Nell* in an *Amazonian* habit," and wound up by a saucy Epilogue archly delivered by the same fair favourite of the town. Such attractions thronged the theatre. Scenting a fit opportunity for malice or revenge, Lady Castle-maine, who always evinced a marked partiality for the King's company and had not disdained to make use of the kindly services of Becky Marshall in her intrigues with handsome Charles Hart, Killigrew's leading man, sent for Mrs. Corey and gave her cer-tain private instructions. At the next performance the actress all through her part cleverly mimicked to the life the oddities of the notorious Lady Harvey, whilst the house fairly rocked with laughter at the jest. Lady Harvey, however, was furious at the impertinence, which was the gossip of both Court and City, and losing no time, she hurried to the Lord Chamberlain, Edward

Montagu, Earl of Manchester, her kinsman, and rattled him up
with such a tale of insult and injury that he incontinently had the
actress arrested and packed off to jail.   Yet the detention was
short enough, for it was at once reported to my Lady Castle-
maine, who without delay ordered the King to set Mrs. Corey
free, and hectored him well nigh out of his wits.   But this was
not enough to satisfy the imperious lady.   A special performance
of *Catiline* was given by royal command, and there before
Charles himself Mrs. Corey repeated her burlesque, broadening
and accentuating every point with a hearty good will, as we may
well believe, to flout and fleer the lady who had given her some
uncomfortable hours in the Gatehouse or Newgate.   At the following performance of Jonson's tragedy when Sempronia appeared she was greeted with a chorus of hisses and cat-calls, and
the air was thick with flying oranges and rotten fruit, which
squelched on the boards and drove the actors for refuge behind
the scenes.   Lady Harvey had hired a whole army of rapscallions
and rowdies, and as these gentry were armed with cold steel as
well as Pomona's bounty, it seemed as if blood might be shed in
the riot which ensued.   " The heat is come to a great height, and
real troubles at Court about it," Pepys gravely observes.   However, Mrs. Corey triumphed, for at this juncture Lady Castle-
maine was " in a higher command over the King than ever—
not as a mistress, for she scorns him, but as a tyrant, to command
him."

The ridiculous introduction of individuals on the stage was a
form of caricature in which a Restoration audience took an
especial delight : the more unmistakable, and often, it must be
confessed, the grosser the personality, the more appreciable the
wit.   As in the theatre of Elizabeth and James I, literary rivals
continually pilloried each other and the critics.   Shadwell had
even dragged Sir Robert Howard across the boards as Sir Positive
Atall, but the most famous example, of course, is Bayes in *The
Rehearsal* when Lacy, dressed in black velvet, Dryden's usual
attire, mimicked the gesture and speech of the laureate to perfection.

A decade later, during the grave political disorders that swirled
about the illegal Exclusion Bill and Oates' Plot, Whig and
Tory loved to scarify their several opponents under names and
shapes that were the merest mockery of disguise, a game at which
the Tories far outdid the dull City faction in talent, point, and

humour. Perhaps this particular kind of satire, which so notably engaged the genius of Aristophanes in England, found its most ardent disciple in Sam Foote, who paid no small price for his burlesques and topical mummery. Nor did the Restoration actor always escape scot-free. On Saturday, January 30th, 1668–9, there was produced at the Theatre Royal *The Heyresse*, a play written by the Duke of Newcastle, with no little assistance, said the gossips, from Dryden. In this new comedy Ned Kynaston dressed his part exactly like the fashionable Sir Charles Sedley, and had the temerity moreover closely to mimic that unscrupulous wit. On the Sunday evening he was waylaid in St. James' Park by a gang of burly ruffians, who, feigning to believe that he was the baronet, thrashed the unlucky youth so severely that for several days he was forced to keep his bed, bruised and sore from head to foot, whilst to the King's angry threats Sedley coolly replied that he had no knowledge whatsoever of the affair. Again on November 4th, 1675, that wicked wag Joe Haines was by a special warrant totally suspended from playing for having " with ill & scandalous language & insolent Carriage " caricatured on the boards " Sir Edmund Windham, his M^{ties} Knight Marshall and His Lady."

On Tuesday, February 9th, 1669, Fletcher's *The Island Princess* was revived at Drury Lane. The action takes place in tropical climes, and thus the play gives much scope for scenic effect, to which particular attention was paid. Some very fine results were obtained, and in the second act the scene of the blazing town of Ternata during the King's night escape from prison is said to have been especially striking. In this revival Mrs. Corey played Quisara, aunt to the Princess Quisara. In 1670 she acted Sophronia in William Joyner's *The Roman Empress*, a somewhat mediocre tragedy, possibly produced as early as the winter of 1669. In the autumn of 1671, probably October, she had a much better part, Mrs. Joyner, the old " Match-maker, or precise City-Bawd," in Wycherley's first comedy, *Love in a Wood*. In the fall of the same year she created Julia in John Corye's *The Generous Enemies*. It does not appear that this dramatist, whose name is indifferently spelled Corye or Cory, was related to the actress.

On Thursday, January 25th, 1672, a terrible calamity befell the King's company in the destruction of the Theatre Royal by fire. A Newsletter, January 27th, 1672, gives the following account : " A fire at the King's playhouse between 7 and 8

o'clock on Thursday evening laſt, which half burned down the
house and all their scenes and wardrobe ; and all the houses
from the Rose Tavern in Russell Street on that side of the way
of Drury Lane are burned and blown up, with many in Vinegar
Yard ; 20,000l. damage.   The fire began under the ſtairs where
Orange Moll keeps her fruit.   Bell the player was blown up."
A ballad on the fire has this couplet :—

> He cryes juſt judgement and wished when poor Bell
> Rung out his laſt, 't been the ſtage's kNell,

lines which for their punning sarcasm on Miſtreſs Gwyn very
nearly got the writer into serious trouble.

Dick Bell himself was a rising young aſtor of great promise.
He was one of those who had been " Bred up from Boys under the
Maſter Aſtors," and at the time of his death could not have been
more than twenty-four years old.   He had originally played such
rôles as Amariel, S. Catherine's Guardian Angel, in Dryden's
Tyrannick Love, or The Royal Martyr, in 1669, and the same year
was excellent as the bandit Strozzo in a notable revival of Shirley's
The Siſters, with Mrs. Knepp as Paulina, the proud siſter ; Mrs.
Hughes, the modeſt siſter Angellina ; their bluff old uncle,
Cartwright ; Prince Farnese, Beeſton ; Lucio, Marmaduke
Watson ; Piperollo, Joe Haines ; and Pulcheria, who is disguised
as Vergerio, a page, Nell Gwyn.   Bell also sustained Julius Cæsar
with Hart as Brutus ; Mohun, Cassius ; and Kynaſton, Mark
Antony.

After the fire the homeless aſtors were glad enough to take
refuge in Davenant's vacant theatre in Lincoln's Inn Fields,
whence the Duke's company had juſt migrated to their magnificent new house in Dorset Gardens, which opened 9 November,
1671, with Dryden's *Sir Martin Mar-All*, a ſtock favourite.   At
Lincoln's Inn Fields Killigrew firſt played a revival of *Wit
without Money* with Mohun as Valentine.   This same year,
1672, the experiment which had been essayed with *The Parson's
Wedding*, nearly a decade before, was repeated, and the women
alone aſted *Philaſter*.   The caſt is not preserved.   In the summer
of 1673 Mrs. Corey appeared as the English Woman in Dryden's
Amboyna.   It is a somewhat melodramatic part with ſtrong
ſtirring speeches which muſt have been very effeſtive.   This
patriotic tragedy met with considerable success.   Critics seem

agreed that it is the poorest of Dryden's plays, yet it is a far better drama than is generally reported, and when we take into consideration that it was planned and written in a month it is surprising how good it is. The treachery of the Dutch, the betrayal of Ysabinda, the villainies in the forest on the wedding night, the torture scenes of Act V, could not but be extremely powerful on the stage. In the same year Mrs. Corey acted Teresa in Duffet's rhyming comedy *The Spanish Rogue*, a curiosity in its way, which was produced *circa* September.

Ever since the date of the all-unfortunate fire there had been almost incessant quarrels and disagreements amongst the members of the King's company, some of whom had gone so far as to transfer their services to the Dorset Gardens Theatre. Meanwhile Killigrew was being recruited by dissatisfied stragglers from his rivals' camp. It was hoped that these difficulties would vanish with the opening on 26 March, 1673-4, of the new Drury Lane Theatre, designed by Sir Christopher Wren, but the feuds persisted with unabated vigour. These abuses in fact increased to such a degree that on 16 May, 1674, Arlington sent an order to the managers to the effect that actors were not to be permitted to go from one house to another in the migratory manner which had grown so common. If they prove contumacious they are " not to be entertained at the Theatres " at all. With regard to Drury Lane, Hart, Mohun, Kynaston and Cartwright were bidden " order and direct all things whatsoever belonging to the well advantage of the Company." That this order did not control the dissentients is proved by the fact that in the spring of 1676 we find Mrs. Marshall and Mrs. Hughes, two actresses of the first rank, playing with Mrs. Barry, Smith, Nokes, and Antony Leigh, in D'Urfey's *A Fond Husband*, which was produced at Dorset Gardens, a comedy so successful that the King himself was present at the first three performances, and must have been fully aware that two of Killigrew's ladies were in the cast. There was ample excuse and indeed reason for their presence,[1] however, for it appeared that the actors at Drury Lane had " left off Actinge upon private differences and disagreements betweene themselves," and a warrant from Arlington, dated February 14th,

---

[1] These two actresses remained some time with the Duke's company and acted several important parts. In 1676 we find Mrs. Hughes as Octavia de Pimentell in Ravenscroft's *The Wrangling Lovers, or The Invisible Mistress*. Leigh, Smith, Underhill, Mrs. Barry and Mrs. Gibbs are in the cast.

1676, required and ordered "the said Company forthwith to
act and play as formerly."

In January, 1674–5, Mrs. Corey appeared as Lucy, a waiting-
maid, in Wycherley's masterpiece of comedy *The Country-Wife*, and
in the winter of 1676 she created that inimitable litigant, the
Widow Blackacre, "the most comical character that was ever
brought upon the stage," in which character she also spoke the
excellent Epilogue to *The Plain-Dealer*. In the spring of 1674 she
played Strega, "an old Rich deformed Lady," the title-rôle of
Duffet's *The Amorous Old Woman*. This beldame, "Mother
Shipton's picture," who has already had seven husbands and is
determined that her eighth shall not wed her merely for the sake
of her wealth, in one farcical scene routs two suitors by taking
off her eyebrows, plucking out an eye, removing her teeth,
shifting her hair, and unscrewing a leg. Finally she is won
by a blind and doting senator, Cicco. In May, 1674, Mrs.
Corey was Agrippina in Lee's first tragedy, *Nero, Emperour
of Rome*. Nero was played by Hart; Britannicus, Mohun;
Petronius, Burt; Otho, Wintershal; Seneca, Cartwright;
Poppea, Mrs. Marshall; Octavia, Betty Cox; Cyara, a Parthian
princess, Mistress of Britannicus, Mrs. Boutell; and the ghost
of Caligula, Philip Griffin; a magnificent cast. Agrippina, it is
true, only appears on the stage, "led by two virgins all in white,"
in the first scene, and the whole part consists of some thirty lines.
But these afford an extraordinarily effective piece of declamation.
In 1675 Mrs. Corey acted Cumana, a priestess of Bellona, in Lee's
heroic drama *Sophonisba; or, Hannibal's Overthrow*. The Hannibal was Mohun, and Sophonisba was taken by Mrs. Cox. In
the spring of 1676 there was a special revival of *A King and No
King*. Mrs. Corey maintained her old rôle of Arane, the Queen-
Mother. About Easter, 1677, Mrs. Corey played the School-
mistress in Ravenscroft's ultra-fantastic farce "after the Italian
manner" *Scaramouch a Philosopher, Harlequin a School-Boy, Bravo,
Merchant, and Magician*. It is a merry piece of tomfoolery, and
the school scene where, under the spectacled Mrs. Philosopher,
armed with giant ferula and rods, Harlequin is found sitting
among the little children stealing slices of bread-and-butter,
munching apples, and conning the Primer, until it closes on a
general birching, is altogether pantomime. Scaramouch was
acted by Philip Griffin, and Joe Haines was Harlequin. Ravenscroft has largely plagiarized *Les Fourberies de Scapin* and *Le*

Mariage Forcé to garnish his droll, but unfortunately for his novelties the Duke's company brought out Otway's *The Cheats of Scapin* a month or two before. He complains bitterly of this " slippery trick " in his Prologue.

In the spring of the same year, 1677, Mrs. Corey acted Sysigambis in Lee's glowing *The Rival Queens ; or, The Death of Alexander the Great*, a tragedy which kept the stage until the middle of the nineteenth century, that is to say, until poetical tragedy ceased to be played. In this drama Hart as Alexander, Mrs. Marshall as Roxana, and Mrs. Boutell as Statira, are acknowledged to have been performances unsurpassed on any stage. In the winter of 1677 Mrs. Corey was Octavia in Dryden's magnificent *All For Love* to the Antony of Hart and Cleopatra of Mrs. Boutell. In the following spring, 1678, she appeared as Quickthrift in *The Man of Newmarket*, the dullest of the Hon. Edward Howard's dull plays.

Between 1678 and 1682 Drury Lane seems largely to have depended upon revivals of the older drama. One reason for this was that Hart and Mohun were growing in years, and both began to suffer from increasing infirmities, which obliged them to play less and less frequently, so that many of their established rôles fell to the lot of the younger actors, such as Cardonell Goodman and Clark, who on their side were all eagerness to seize upon the chief parts, and who often proved exceedingly intractable in the first flush of some new success. In the early spring of 1682 was produced Southerne's earliest tragedy, *The Loyal Brother ; or, The Persian Prince*, whose plot, taken from a famous novel, which had been translated in 1676 by P. Porter as *Tachmas, Prince of Persia*, was chosen in compliment to the Duke of York. Seliman, the Sophy of Persia, was acted by Goodman ; Tachmas, his loyal brother, by Clark ; Ismael, the villain, Mohun ; Begona, the Queen-Mother, Mrs. Corey ; Semanthe, whom Tachmas loves, Sarah Cook ; Sunamire, who secretly loves Tachmas, Anne Quin.

Negotiations, however, were in progress during that year with reference to an amalgamation between the two theatres, and, after considerable delay and much heart-burning and jealousy, the Duke's actors removed from Dorset Gardens to Drury Lane, where the united companies opened on 16 November, 1682, a Prologue being written by Dryden and spoken by Betterton. The King and Queen attended in state, and the house was

crowded with a brilliant audience.   Charles Hart, now seriously
ill with ftone and gravel, had already retired, and Mohun's
name occurs very rarely after this date.   Hart died of ftone at
his country house at Stanmore Magna, Middlesex, and was
buried there, 20 Auguft, 1683.   Mohun died in Brownlow
Street, now Betterton Street, Drury Lane, in October, 1684, and
is buried in S. Giles-in-the-Fields.

In the early autumn of 1683 Mrs. Corey created Dame Dobson
in Ravenscroft's " recantation play," *Dame Dobson ; or, The
Cunning Woman*, an English version of *La Devineresse ; ou, Les
aux Enchantements* (sometimes known as *Madame Jobin*), a capital
comedy by Thomas Corneille and Jean Donneau de Vise.   This
French original had been produced in 1679, and both the ftage-
craft and the adroit way in which the various tricks and conjurations are managed muft be allowed to be consummately
clever.   An English comedy on a similar theme is *The Wise-
Woman of Hogsdon*, the intricacies of which are a triumph of
technique.   But *Dame Dobson* and *La Devineresse* are alike
entirely lacking in the romantic poetry and moments of rare
beauty which inveft Heywood's play with its gracious springtide
charm.   *La Devineresse* was published in 1680, and the address
" Au lecteur " commences thus : " Le succès de cette Comédie
a efté si grand, qu'il s'en eft peu veu de semblables.   On y a
couru, et on y court encor tous les jours en foule."   The little
book has a frontispiece picturing a grimalkin, a hand of glory,
noxious weeds, two blazing torches, and other objects beloved
of necromancy.   There are moreover eight folding plates of
great intereft representing scenes in the play.   Unfortunately
on the English ftage *Dame Dobson* met with little success, much
less indeed than it deserved.   In the spring of 1684 Mrs. Corey
acted Mrs. Trainwell, Conftance's governess, in a revival of
Brome's *The Northern Lasse*.   The same year she created Angellina's mother in Southerne's highly amusing comedy *The Dis-
appointment ; or, The Mother in Fashion*, to the Rogero of Anthony
Leigh.   In the summer of 1685 she played Roselia, Protectress
of the Amazonian country, in D'Urfey's meddlesome alteration
of *The Sea Voyage*.   *Circa* September of the same year we find
her as Mrs. Touchftone, the goldsmith's wife, in *Cuckold's-
Haven ; or, An Alderman no Conjurer*, a version of *Eaftward Hoe*
due to Nahum Tate.   Although some of his broadly farcical
scenes are comic to a degree, Tate cannot be said to have improved

his original. Touchstone, for example, becomes little better than a buffoon. This rôle was intended for Nokes, but when he was accidentally prevented from playing (probably by a sudden illness), it had to be taken at the last minute by Percival. Jevon acted Quicksilver, the idle 'prentice ; Leigh, Security ; and Joe Haines, Bramble. In January, 1686, was produced *The Banditti*, an excellent comedy by D'Urfey, which owes something however to Shirley's *The Sisters*. Mrs. Corey acted Eugenia ; Mrs. Barry, Laura, her daughter ; and the house roared with laughter at Nokes in petticoats as Megaera, the wife of the brigand chief.

In the spring of 1687 Mrs. Behn's delightful pantomimic farce *The Emperor of the Moon* was produced at Dorset Garden with unbounded applause. Mrs. Corey played Mopsophil the Governante, whose hand is sought by Scaramouch (Leigh) and Harlequin (Jevon). Cave Underhill appeared as the old doctor.

In May, 1688, Shadwell's *The Squire of Alsatia* drew the whole town to Drury Lane. " The House," writes the dramatist, " was never so full since it was built." Mrs. Corey was seen as Ruth, a precise old duenna with a silver strong-water bottle in her pocket. Early in 1689 some trouble had arisen in the playhouse, and Mrs. Corey was excluded, since we find her petitioning the Lord Chamberlain on March 11th of that year for readmittance, and an order was sent for her to be at once allowed to return. In April she acted in another of Shadwell's comedies, the bustling *Bury-Fair*. Her rôle was Lady Fantast, who has bred up her daughter a wit and a linguist of a kind. In the winter she played Farmosa in *The Successful Strangers*, a brisk comedy by handsome Will Mountfort, the ladies' favourite. In November she created Mrs. Flirt, the tapstress, an amusing part in Mrs. Behn's posthumous play *The Widdow Ranter*, which, having already been something maltreated by George Jenkins, who revised the script, was " murdered " in the performance.

In the later winter, December, of 1689,[1] D'Urfey's *Love for Money ; or, The Boarding School*, an excellent comedy of which the scene is Chelsea by the river, caused considerable scandal by

---

[1] It should be remarked that our eminent theatrical authority Mr. W. J. Lawrence dates this production *circa* July—November, 1690. The play is sharply satirized in *Wit for Money, or Poet Stutter*, which is advertised in the *Term Catalogues*, Easter (May), 1691. D'Urfey says that *Love for Money* was written in June, 1689.

E.P.

its reflections on the banished monarch and the loyalists in the person of Lady Addleplot, a character made doubly grotesque by the clowning of Leigh in ample skirts and rigid busk. The school scenes with the romps are extremely good. Mrs. Corey played Mrs. Crowstick, teacher to the Boarding School.

In the spring of 1690 Belliza in Shadwell's *The Amorous Bigotte* supplied Mrs. Corey with a good character albeit farcical. Belliza, who is spasmodically wooed by Bernardo, a vapouring old colonel, alternates between ancient coquetries when he visits her and, when he cools, exercises of piety under the direction of Teague O'Divelly, an Irish friar, an outrageous caricature, played by Anthony Leigh. In October, 1690, Mrs. Corey acted Bromia, the shrewish wife of Sosia, in *Amphitryon*, a comedy in which Dryden has easily equalled, if not indeed surpassed, both Plautus and Molière. One such masterpiece alone would suffice to place this great poet in the very front rank of our dramatists. In the late winter, probably December, Shadwell's boisterous *The Scowrers* was produced with Mountfort as the rakehelly young hero ; Joe Williams and Leigh, Wildfire and bottle-nosed Tope, his boon companions ; Mrs. Leigh, the amorous but truculent Lady Maggot ; Mrs. Barry and Mrs. Bracegirdle, Eugenia and Clara ; and Mrs. Corey, Priscilla, their governess. It is a thoroughly laughable, noisy, unruly, mohocking play, and all goes with great verve and spirit. But however pleasant on the stage, the "scowrers" were blackguardly nuisances in the streets.

In March, 1691, Mountfort's *Greenwich Park* was received with particular favour by his many admirers. It is a very commendable piece of work, inspired in some sort by Sedley, Wycherley, and Etherege. Mrs. Corey appeared as the Aunt to Dorinda. In the spring of the same year was produced D'Urfey's *Bussy D'Ambois ; or, The Husband's Revenge*, an alteration of Chapman. In the days of Hart, " that eternally renowned and best of actors," who had played the hero with wonderful vigour and grace, Chapman's tragedy was always well received, but since the death of the one and only Bussy the piece " lay buried in [his] grave " in the quiet churchyard of Stanmore Magna. It was with no small difficulty indeed that D'Urfey persuaded Mountfort to undertake the rôle, so overshadowed did he feel by his great predecessor. Mrs. Bracegirdle acted Tamyra, and Mrs. Corey was Teresia, her confidante, whom D'Urfey has wisely substituted for Friar Comolet. In fact the whole revision is done with much skill, and in many ways the rough-hewn scenes are vastly improved. The revival won the notable success it well merited. In December, 1691, Mrs. Corey created Mrs. Teazall in Southerne's admirable *The Wives Excuse ; or, Cuckolds Make Themselves*, a play which earned an immortal compliment from Dryden. Mrs. Teazall, who is much exercised about the morals of her niece Fanny, a young lady given to frequent very undesirable company on the sly, is a marvellous creation. Her passion for cards, her bustling flurried ways, her volubility, her plain speaking, which overflows in a torrent of priceless Billingsgate when she denounces the wicked ways of living in the town, are all drawn by the hand of a master. In January, 1691–2, she also had an excellent character in D'Urfey's *The Marriage Hater Matched*, a first-rate comedy, which gained unbounded applause. It was acted six times in succession, a good run for those days, and herein Dogget first definitely made his mark as a comedian of superlative gifts. The scene is the Park, near Kensington. The cast was extremely strong. Mrs. Corey played My Lady Bumfiddle, " A Prating, Matchmaking, Eating, Impertinent Creature, visiting everyone for the sake of a good Dinner, and always teizing 'em with fulsome Stories of the Intrigues about the Town," a very modern type.

In March, 1692, was revived *The Traitor*, a tragedy forthwith reprinted " with Alterations & Amendments," which are merely the few slight omissions of the prompt-book. There was at the time something more than a tradition that this noble tragedy was the work of Antony Rivers, a Jesuit priest, who wrote it during his imprisonment in Newgate, where he died. The author is stated to have handed his manuscript to Shirley, who, with his intimate knowledge of things theatrical, revised the scenes and brought them on to the stage. It is very obvious that a drama known to be the composition of a Jesuit would have been heavily handicapped, in fact foredoomed to failure, whilst any play by so popular a favourite as Shirley would have at least had a favourable hearing. Shirley himself was a Catholic, and there can be little doubt that the story is substantially true. Nason in his *Study of Shirley*, a painstaking but uninspired volume, refers to but hardly discusses the point, and R. S. Forsythe in his somewhat arid *Shirley's Plays and the Elizabethan Drama* treats it far too cursorily. Dyce's opinion is so bitterly prejudiced as to be negligible. Nor can it be argued that Atkins' verses carry weight, for at the time the secret was no doubt inviolably kept. In fine, the ascription of *The Traitor* primarily to Rivers may be with due reservations definitely accepted. The plot of this fine drama treats (with variations from historical fact) the story of the assassination of Duke Alessandro de Medici by his cousin Lorenzino, a theme so ably handled in De Musset's *Lorenzaccio*. The Duke was acted by Robert Hudson ; Lorenzo, Kynaston ; Sciarrha, Joseph Williams ; Pisano, Colley Cibber ; Depazzi, Haines ; Rogero, the page-boy, Tommy Kent ; Oriana, Mrs. Lassells ; Amidea, Anne Bracegirdle ; and her old mother Morossa, Mrs. Corey. *The Traitor* had a tremendous ovation. The same year, 1692, saw another revival : *The Merry Devil of Edmonton*—that " dear little drama," as it has been called, a play full of love, romantic friendship, and sympathy, truly tender and sweet, whose scenes are fresh and pure as the country-side and the fragrant dawn of which they treat. Betterton acted Sir Ralph Jerningham ; Mountfort, Raymond Mounchensey ; Nokes, Sir John ; Leigh, the Host ; Kynaston, the warlock Fabel ; Mrs. Leigh, Lady Clare ; Mrs. Bracegirdle, Millicent ; and Mrs. Corey, the Abbess of Cheston.

The fall of 1692 proved a sad winter for the theatre. On the night of December 9th poor Will Mountfort was foully assassinated in Norfolk Street, Strand, by two dastardly scoundrels, Captain Richard Hill and Lord Mohun, who presumed to be jealous of his intimacy with Mrs. Bracegirdle. Within a week James Nokes died of a malignant fever, and Anthony Leigh did not survive his old comrade many days. After this year Mrs. Corey's name does not appear in the casts. It seems that her parts were forthwith assigned to Mrs. Leigh. This lady's salary since the death of her husband, the Patentees declared in their famous paper of December 10th, 1694, had been raised 10*s*., so that she was in receipt of 30*s*., and this (they say) was all that the popular Mrs. Corey ever was paid. There is no record, however, of Mrs. Corey's death, and such being the case, we may at least hope, if not assert, that she retired to enjoy some years of ease and leisure after so long, so brilliant, and so interesting a career.

ORRERY'S "THE TRAGEDY OF ZOROASTRES"

ORRERY'S "THE TRAGEDY OF ZOROASTRES"

ALTHOUGH Roger Boyle, Earl of Orrery, is an important figure in our dramatic literature, not so much perhaps from any outstanding poetical merit as from his position as the pioneer and a prominent purveyor of heroic tragedy, it will be found that the history and bibliography of his theatre have up to the present time been by no means clearly presented, but that several points which care and research might have elucidated are left doubtful and obscure. Quite recent discovery has indeed finally settled the vexed question as to the originator of the rhymed heroic drama in England and, by proving that Orrery was the first to use the rhymed couplet in this fashion, emphasized the point and pertinency of Dryden's dedication to *The Rival Ladies* (4to, 1664), showing that his address and the defence of " following the New way . . . of writing Scenes in Verse " are no mere partial phrase and compliment, as many critics have thought, but must be taken to be literally and definitely true.

The collected edition of Orrery's works, 2 vols., 1739, " for R. Dodsley in Pall Mall," unfortunately enough excludes his comedy *Mr. Anthony* (4to, 1690),[1] and gives in its place the somewhat insipid *As You Find It*[2] by Charles Boyle. There seems no reason for this eclecticism, save the carelessness or caprice of the editor, but we are accordingly not surprised to find that he did not trouble to print—even if he were cognizant of its existence—Orrery's last work, *The Tragedy of Zoroastres*, which still remains in MS. (*Sloane*, 1828), unedited and practically unknown. Clarence in *The Stage Cyclopaedia* has, it is true, duly noted this play, but we find no mention of it in *The Dictionary of National Biography*, in *The Cambridge History of English Literature*, Vol. VIII, nor yet in Ward, nor in Nettleton. As it has never been printed and is almost totally forgotten there should be an account of this strange and, in some ways, representative play.

---

[1] Produced about twenty years before.
[2] Produced at Lincoln's Inn Fields in April, 1703 ; 4to, 1703.

The Tragedy of Zoroastres, which bears as a motto Ovid's line " Omne genus Scripti grauitate Tragoedia uincit " (*Tristia*, II, 381), and the Horatian " Scribimus indoćti doćtiq.—" (*Ep*. II, 1, 117), has inscribed beneath the title " Written in 1676." There seems no reason to dispute this date, about which time Orrery was living in the south of Ireland. The dramatis personae are set out as follows :

The Persons Names	Represented by
Zoroaśtres King of Baćtria yᵉ firśt Magician [1]	
Oroandes Young King of Armenia	Ally's to
Phylander Prince of Macedon	Zoroaśtres
Daemolgoron son to Zoroaśtres	

Woemen

Juliana } Polynice } Daughters to Zoroaśtres	
Cyane Phylander's siśter	
Trivia Governess to yᵉ 2 Princesses	
High Prieśt Ambassadour	
Guards	
Spirits	
Ghośt	
Attendants	

The Scaen Baćtria

There is neither Prologue nor Epilogue, a faćt which together with the absence of performers' names I shall notice later.

The firśt aćt opens with " The scene a dark grove on yᵉ side of a Rock, at yᵉ bottom yᵉ Ocean with ships riding is seen, out of the grove Zoroaśtres comes attended severall spirits ascending and meeting him, all with burning lamps in their hands, śtrange sort of Noises are heard in the air with flashes of lightning & thunder. Zoroaśtres comes forward & speakes :

K. How great's my Pow'r ?   Whose hand Hell's throne can shake
    And Drousey Ghośts from beds of Earth awake.
    Pluto himself does frightnd Trembling śtand
    And dreads his Treasure when I wave my wand."

[1] This tradition is mentioned by very many authors.   Cf. Pliny, *Hiśtoria Naturalis*, xxx, 2 : Ars magica " sine dubio illic orta in Perside a Zoroastre, ut inter aućtores conuenit."   By some Zoroaster was identified with Cham (Ham), the son of Noah. Cf. *Réalité de la Magie*, Paris, 1819, pp. 12, 13.   Sixtus of Siena (d. 1569), the famous Dominican theologian, says there were two magicians of the name Zoroaster ; the one, King of Persia, was the author of natural magic ; the other, King of Baćtria, invented black magic and demonolatry.

Experience goes to show that the old authors seldom wrote elaborate stage-directions, and that these were generally added by the prompter. (This must not of course be taken as applying to semi-operatic and spectacular performances.) Orrery however was a striking exception to this rule, and the opening direction here may be paralleled with that in *Henry the Fifth* (1664) at the commencement of Act IV, and again with the elaborate scenario of *The Black Prince*, produced 19 Oct., 1667. These were smartly parodied by Buckingham (see my edition of *The Rehearsal*, p. 137). A back-cloth of the ocean or a river with ships was a favourite set in heroic tragedies, doubtless as affording a stately prospect and giving scope to the scene-painter; cf. John Webb's design for Davenant's *Siege of Rhodes*, I, 1 (Chatsworth collection, box A, drawing No. 13 (*b*)), of which a reproduction is given in *The Burlington Magazine*, May, 1914. So we have in *The Rival Ladies*, Act IV, "Scene the Third. *Through a Rock is discover'd a Navy of Ships Riding at a Distance*"; in Settle's *The Empress of Morocco*, Act II, 1, "*The Scene opened, is represented the Prospect of a large River, with a glorious Fleet of Ships, supposed to be the Navy of* Muly Hamet." [1]

Zoroaster dismisses his Spirits, and as they depart he spies his son, Daemolgoron, walking in a grove,

Melancholy, as if hee were in Love.

In a few moments he overhears him confess his love for Cyane, and at the same time his fear to avow it. Daemolgoron "falls in a Trance on a Couch" and the King, cursing his passion, and resolving to "tare him from her Arms," goes out. Thereupon "Two spirits in shapes of woemen clad all in white with Wands fly down and stand before Daemol: who all ye while lays asleep on a Couch." They sing and invoke Cupid, who appears "brandishing a dart, ye 2 spirits fly up to him. And on a sudden ye stage darkens & ye cave and grove vanish." The scene then "shifts into a Pallace." Oroandes and Phylander enter. In sonorous lines—amongst the best in the play—Oroandes declares his eagerness for action and war. Proud Persia who is last "to adore ye Rising Sun" must be subdued. Phylander asserts his darling wish to follow Oroandes, when they are interrupted by Juliana

---

[1] It is interesting to compare the engraving of this scene in *The Empress of Morocco*, 4to, 1673, with Gravelot's illustration (*G. Vᵃʳ Gucht Scul.*) to *The Rival Ladies*, which depicts IV, 3, of that play.

and Polynice, who are seen " hand in hand at yᵉ other end of yᵉ
Stage." Phylander falls into a rapture, but Oroandes tries to drag
him away, shouting " To War—to War ! " " Whilest Phylander
stands talking to himself yᵉ two princesses goe of yᵉ stage as hee
goes to follow 'em two Cupids fly down & stand before him One
Like a handsome boy yᵉ other a Young Girl." These aerial
visitants sing, and the Girl says :

> The smallest hair I have shall bee thy Chain
> And you shall liue my slaue whilst I doe Reign.

They then vanish. It is impossible here but to be reminded of
Pope's " And beauty draws us with a single hair," *The Rape of
the Lock*, II, 28. Scenes in which spirits descend and sing were
frequent in the heroic drama, and are prime favourites with
Orrery. One may refer to the beginning of the Second Act of
The Black Prince for a salient example. Presently Juliana and
Polynice re-enter to Phylander, who wishes to retire since

> Our Ancient Bards did write men ought to dye
> And they approach'd Diuinity too nigh.

Upon a little encouragement however he tells his name :

> My Name's Phylander & my father Reigns
> Ouer yᵉ Great & large Pharsalian Plains
> Renown'd for Battles——,

and even proceeds to declare love to Polynice. She is now mild,
now imperious, but lingers until summoned thence by Trivia.
Oroandes returns and expostulates with his friend, terming him
a " Heretick to War." The scene next " shifts to a pleasant
Orange Grove " where we find Cyane endeavouring to avoid
Daemolgoron, who follows her crying " Divine ! Adored ! "
She repulses him, and a little later when he confesses to his father
his love, Zoroastres abruptly replies :

> As long as you a Passion for her own
> You'll loose your Title to your Father's Crown.

Act II opens with another spectacle of spirits and amorini.
" The scene drawn. Oroandes is discouer'd laying asleep uppon
a Couch." A vision appears of the Temple of Cupid, who
descends " with 2 darts in his hands, one of Jealousey, yᵉ other
of despair, hee goes round Oroandes at last sticks 'em both in

him." A song is given for Cupid " How sweet is revenge to our Godship above," and in his dream Oroandes sees Polynice, smiling and beautiful. He wakes, and, in lines that out-Herod the wildest rants of Maximin or Almanzor, raves of his passion for this bright nymph. Polynice enters, and in a furious scene the hero swears " by all th' innumerous gods " that he loves her. Rejecting his suit she coldly leaves him to despair. In the next scene, the Palace, Zoroastres rebuffs the Persian ambassador and declares war. There is " a noise of drums & hollowing," and the King encourages the princes to arm for battle. As Polynice bids a tender farewell to Phylander, Oroandes overhears them. Juliana and Cyane enter, and Juliana reveals to Oroandes that she loves him, upon which Cyane cries :

> What shall I doe, I am for ever lost
> My Loue must needs bee by ye Princess crost
> His Nature's too soe haughty and seuere
> That my Complaints and sighs hee'le never hear.
> Then to my dying howr I will conceal,
> And ne're that I a lover was reveal.

Meanwhile a warlike noise, heard at first " afar off," gets louder and louder, and is explained to be the King at the head of his warriors going to the temple of the God of War :

> This day for solemn rites hee does approve
> To Morrow towards Persia they doe move.

Immediately " Enter King Zor : Daemolgoron, Phylander Cyane with Preists holding Wands. The scene Mars' Temple at ye foot of the Altar Tapers stand burning with dishes of blood. The Divan or High Preist takes a dish of blood and after ye Ceremony speaks " :

> This blood the fates from dying Persia took
> And at ye blow th' expiring kingdome shook.

Anon Daemolgoron prophesies the doom of Persia :

> The swelling Granick flood shall bloody run
> With sanguine streams and fright their setting sun.
> With raging Flames wee'le all their Citys burn
> The very Heau'ns with smoke shall clouded turn.
> All their high marble tow'rs shall scorchèd bee ⎫
> Soe much of fire Persia then shall see   ⎬
> That she shall mistake her own Deity   ⎭

With this we may compare *The Rival Queens*, Act II, 1, where Alexander cries :

> Can none remember ? Yes, I know all must
> When Glory, like the dazzling Eagle, stood
> Perch'd on my Bever in the *Granick* Flood ;
> When Fortune's self my Standard trembling bore,
> And the pale Fates stood frighted on the Shore.

Lee, of course, attains heights of poetry and majestic grandiloquence to which Orrery could never reach.

Zoroastres promises Polynice to the Prince who achieves the most heroic deed in the war, which gives occasion for Oroandes and Phylander to proclaim their rivalry. The procession of courtiers and priests passes on, and Juliana left alone with Oroandes loads him with reproaches, screaming out :

> Outriual'd by my sister ?—Yonger too ?
> Curse on my stars !

To her accusations of falseness he replies in chilling accents :

> Madam you said you'de not accept of mine,
> You bawk'd my flame which did soe glorious shine,
> Thank then your self——

He leaves her, and we have a dance of Salii with a martial song " Feirce War, Feirce War is a coming." Six spirits then rise and " dance an Antick dance," which ended, the scene changes to the orange grove. Zoroastres enters, exclaiming

> Soe now I'le satisfye my love, my son
> Who is my rivall, I have sent to wars.
> For I must own it, that Cyane's beauty
> Has surprised mee.
> And heated my age into feircest loue.   Bowes to
> But lest you Beautys should think this a sin   ye Boxes.
> Though age without Thanke joue I'ue youth within.   shakes
>   himself.

Cyane appears " at ye other end of ye Walk." Zoroastres declares his love. The lady spurns and defies him, and there is much bombast. The act ends with a tag spoken by the King :

> Remember Gallants that you have been told
> You'de better loue when Young then when you're old.

In the MS. a fresh hand commences at the line " And heated

my age . . ." continuing to the end of the play.   The passage of
direct appeal to the audience is most noticeable.   It may be
paralleled in the Elizabethan drama, but I know of no instance
occurring in a play of so late a date as *Zoroastres*.   Brome indeed
in *The Antipodes* (acted at Salisbury Court in 1638), has a sneer
at such conventions :

> *Letoy.*   when you are
> To speake to your coactors in the Scene,
> You hold interloquutions with the Audients.
>
> *Byplay.*   That is a way my Lord has bin allow'd
> On elder stages to move mirth and laughter.
>
> *Let.*   Yes in the dayes of *Tarlton* and *Kempe*,
> Before the stage was purg'd from barbarisme,
> And brought to the perfection it now shines with.

" Thanke joue " originally stood " Thanke God." The word
" God " has been deleted and " joue " is written over the line.

Act III opens with a garden.   Juliana in fine frenzy is raving
of her love for Oroandes.   Trivia attempts to comfort her.
Zoroastres enters with his attendants.   He sends for Cyane,
" Meanwhile he sits down. soft Musick aboue."   Cyane again
rejects his suit, and enraged he swears :

> By Burning Stix I'le have thy life or Loue.
> Guards ! seize that Witch there.

She is seized, but in a few moments the amorous king falls at
her feet imploring mercy for his cruelty.   In the next scene
Juliana reproaches Polynice for having gained Oroandes' love.
Polynice assures her that he has no place in her heart.   " The
scene changes.   Cyane is discouered laying on a Couch with a
book in her hand.   Two Tapers burning by her.   A Terrible
Clap of Thunder is heard.   Seuerall streams of fire cross y^e
stage & ye heavens open from which a spirit descends, and sings "

> Song.
> From Orosmades ye great
> And from Alha lord of fate
> To you bright Beauty am I come
> To tell you your approaching doom.

As Cyane wakes, Zoroastres enters with a poison'd bowl.   Since
she still treats him with contumely, he compels her to drink,
and she incontinently expires cursing the tyrant.

In *The Rival Queens*, II, 1, we also find a mention of Orosmades, where Aristander, the soothsayer, announces the omens of ill:

To *Orosmades'* Cave I did repair,
Where I aton'd the dreadful God with prayer.

A triumph opens Act IV. "The scene Bactria. ye streets all hung with rich Tapestry in which may be represented ye wars & Overthrow of Persia. after severall sorts of Musick heard and acclamations Daemolgoron and ye 2 Princes enter through a guard of souldiers the Captives following them with their sword points downward " Zoroastres and his court meet the victors. Both Phylander, who has twice saved Daemolgoron's life, and Oroandes, who has killed the Persian king in single combat, demand the hand of the princess. Zoroastres puts them off for a while, and meantime bestows the Kingdom of Persia on Oroandes. When Zoroastres is alone " severall spirits arise all in black with ghastly vizards." He sends them to secure the two princes by enchantment:

Use all your pow'rfull drugs that may them keep,
Try watchfull life to Captive with your sleep.
Secure their body's, then cast Magick round,
And that noe place at all for flight be found
Let all ye world bee made inchanted ground.

The scene changes to a " Rock with woods adjoyning. Enter Oroandes following ye shape of Polynice who still flys from him." A moment or two after, three savages lead her swiftly across the stage " into one of the alleys." She cries for help, and Oroandes " pursues them to a caue which is at ye foot of ye rock, they all vanish and leave him chain'd dancing round him." The prince finds he can stir neither hand nor foot. Next Phylander is entrapped by precisely the same business and the same magic glamour. He is bound in a circle opposite to Oroandes. Daemolgoron has discovered Cyane's murder, and when the scene shuts on the two captives he rushes in with drawn sword threatening his father. " Soft Musick is heard aboue. ye heavens open Cyane descends all pale, four Cupids hang ore her head weeping, crown'd with Cypress Garlands." As Daemolgoron gazes she ascends to soft music. This vision is very similar to that of Rosalinda in Lee's *Sophonisba ; or, Hannibal's Overthrow*, produced at Drury Lane in the spring of 1675.

Hannibal has had recourse to the priestesses of Bellona, who by their horrid rites show him the future, and "Rosalinda *rises in a Chair, pale, with a Wound on her breast; two* Cupids *descend, and hang weeping over her."*

Zoroastres is seen talking to the two ensorcelled captives who defy him even in their chains. He shouts :

> By Asmenoth ! you shall both dye, Appear
> My guardian spirits.

The demons go out muttering and return with Cyane's head which they hold "against Phylanders face." The scene shuts on this ghoulish fantasy, and Zoroastres remains alone. Daemolgoron with a troop of soldiers appears and is about to make the King prisoner. The wizard monarch summons his spirits, but to his dismay the genius answers :

> Thy Power, O King, is now expir'd !
> I open'd ye Golden Legend & there saw
> Thy leas'd soul run out & forfeited.

At the same moment a messenger, half-distraught, rushes in crying that the palace is in flames, the mighty statue of Zoroastres has fallen and is broken to pieces, whilst innumerable spirits are to be seen mingled with the fire, exulting in the ruin. "The scene shifts to ye Rocks where ye Princes were chain'd. their chains drop of & ye spirits vanish."

At the commencement of Act V we find Juliana, Polynice and Trivia in a state of terrible fear. Polynice declares :

> The Sibill's now fulfill'd wee must expire
> And all our world must perish in this fire.

Temples, houses, streets blaze amain. (From this point the play deserts rhyme for halting blank verse.) The High Priest enters robed in full pontificals and summons the spirit Ariell, who announces that Zoroastres must die, and of the royal house only Polynice will be left alive to be happy with Phylander. In a short passage Daemolgoron and his soldiers cry out for the King's death. Here is a brief lyric interlude, a song of spirits headed by Ariell. The palace is shown. Zoroastres, crowned, in his most splendid attire, defiant, is seated on his throne. Daemolgoron is dragged in fettered. On a sudden thunder peals, lightning flashes, and "streams of fire cross ye stage."

Furies and demons arise shaking dark torches at the monarch.
They howl a chorus of doom, and in a moment " all descend,
pulling yᵉ King down with them, yᵉ Heavens raining fire uppon
them." A grove closes over these horrors. Oroandes enters,
to whom Trivia brings the news of Juliana's death. The
prince in a few tame lines remarks that he will leave Bactria for
ever :

> Hence then to Camps and Bloody feilds I'le goe
> Where Death does reign and all Mankind's my foe.

In the last scene we have a magnificent temple. The nuptials
of Phylander and Polynice are in progress. The High Priest
invokes Ariell who descends " clad all in white " and blesses the
happy pair.

It would seem that Orrery did not trouble to gather up his
threads in this last act. We hear nothing of Daemolgoron, who
was made prisoner when attempting his father's life, save a
casual line from Polynice to the effect that her brother is dead.
The fate of Juliana and the departure of Oroandes are most
confusedly and badly told.

It certainly cannot be claimed that *The Tragedy of Zoroastres*
has any great literary value. It is in truth easily the worst of
Orrery's dramas, but from its very roughness and the huddled
conclusion I am strongly inclined to think that what we possess
is merely an unrevised copy, lacking the author's final touches
and polish. That the Horatian canon with regard to diction is
flagrantly violated, that we have *ampullas et sesquipedalia uerba*
followed by the most impertinent *sermo pedestris*, is not matter
for surprise, hardly for criticism ; only the very greatest writers
of heroic drama could escape this pitfall, perhaps none save Dryden
himself. On the stage however the scene of Zoroastres' doom
would have been very effective, and with all his faults Orrery had
a keen eye for theatrical effect, a gift that more than once won
him success when the tragedy of far greater and purer writers
failed. Even in his comedy *Guzman* he could not refrain from
giving us an elaborate scene in an " astrological cabinet," where,
although the magic is feigned, we have spells and conjurations,
a boy drest as a baboon, another as the devil, Maria, Lucia, and
their maids in glittering habits presenting aerial spirits and genii,
together with an abundance of " great flashes of fire."

It seems improbable that *The Tragedy of Zoroastres* was actually

played.   The facts that no Prologue nor Epilogue is given, that
" Represented by " is followed by a blank, are almost conclusive
on this point.   It was probably prepared for the old Smock
Alley Theatre, Dublin, which in the Post-Restoration period had
a music gallery over the proscenium, similar to the music loft
at the Duke's in Dorset Garden, shown in an illustration to
Act I, 1, of Settle's *The Empress of Morocco* (4to, 1673).   This
would account for the stage-direction " music above " which
so frequently occurs in Orrery's play.   Unfortunately the Irish
theatrical annals of that period have not come down to us, so
whilst at present we are able to state it as a strong probability that
The Tragedy of Zoroastres never saw the boards, we must yet
hesitate to assert this as an undisputed and incontrovertible fact.

THE SOURCE OF SOUTHERNE'S
"THE FATAL MARRIAGE"

THE SOURCE OF SOUTHERNE'S
"THE FATAL MARRIAGE"

IN the Epistle Dedicatory to Antony Hammond, Esq., of Somersham-Place, prefacing that pathetic tragedy *The Fatal Marriage ; or The Innocent Adultery* [1] (4to, 1694), Southerne writes " I took the Hint of the Tragical part of this Play from a Novel of Mrs *Behn's* call'd *The Fair Vow-Breaker ;* you will forgive me for calling it a Hint, when you find I have little more than borrow'd the Question how far such a Distress was to be carry'd upon the Misfortune of a Woman's having innocently two Husbands at the same time."

It has up till now been confidently and repeatedly asserted that *The Fair Vow-Breaker* (or to give the novel its full title, *The Nun ; or, The Fair Vow-Breaker*) is the name under which Mrs. Behn's *The Nun ; or, The Perjur'd Beauty*, a story to be found in all the collected editions of her Histories and Novels, first appeared in a separate *editio princeps*, 12mo, 1689. This is definitely stated by Miss Charlotte E. Morgan in her monograph *The Rise of the Novel of Manners* (The Columbia University Press, 1911), who when speaking of *The Nun ; or, The Perjur'd Beauty*, appends a footnote : " *History of the Nun, or, The Faire Vow Breaker*, was the title of the first edition, 1689 " (p. 83) ; and again on page 201 under the date 1689 she catalogues : " *The History of the Nun ; or the Fair Vow Breaker. By Aphra Behn.* Reprinted in her collected works as *The Perjur'd Beauty.*" Mr. A. T. Bartholomew in *The Cambridge History of English Literature*, Vol. VIII (1912), Chapter VII, The Restoration Drama, III, Tragic Poets, writing of Southerne has as follows : " It was not until 1694 that, in *The Fatal Marriage ; or, The Innocent Adultery*, he achieved a play worthy of his talent. This popular drama was

---

[1] This has nothing to do with Scarron's novel *L'Innocent Adultère* which translated was so popular in the seventeenth and eighteenth centuries. Bellmour carried it in his pocket when he went a-courting Laetitia and horrified old Fondlewife who found it (*The Old Batchelor*, 1693). Lydia Languish was partial to its perusal in 1775. Sir A. W. Ward mistakenly assumes that it was Southerne's tragedy she borrowed from the Bath circulating library.

founded on Mrs. Aphra Behn's novel *The Nun ; or, The Perjur'd Beauty.*"

Before Miss Morgan and Mr. Bartholomew, such recognized scholars as Sir A. W. Ward, first in his *History of Dramatic Literature*, Vol. III, p. 421 (1899), secondly in his article on Southerne in the *Dictionary of National Biography ;* and Joseph Knight in his *David Garrick* (1894) had lent the sanction of their undisputed authority to the above, which has so long been recognized and amply accepted. The fact is that *The Nun ; or, The Perjur'd Beauty* had not been thoroughly examined in connexion with *The Fatal Marriage*. When this was done a serious discrepancy was soon seen to exist. The plot of the novel has literally nothing in common with Southerne's tragedy. It deals indeed with the intrigues of a certain Ardelia, a mere coquette, who by her wicked trifling with three different men is responsible for the severing of friendships and no less than five deaths ; her lovers', Elvira's and her own. Isabella, Southerne's heroine, on the other hand, falls a sad victim to the dastardly machinations of Carlos, her black-hearted brother-in-law. She is virtuous and a mirror of constancy ; Ardelia is a jade capable of the most callous treachery. Both novel and play end tragically, it is true, but from different motives and in a totally dissimilar manner. The title indeed, *The Nun*, is really a misnomer unless we are by that to understand Elvira, a secondary character in the tale, which can hardly be. Ardelia never takes the veil. Having befooled Don Antonio and embroiled him with Henrique, she retires to a cloister but merely as a parlour boarder, and she meets her fate in the convent garden when on the point of eloping with Sebastian. Southerne's Isabella is a professed nun who has violated her vows and abandoned enclosure [1] for love of Biron ; a very different state of affairs.

The crux then is what exactly did Southerne mean by the " Hint " he borrowed from " a Novel of Mrs Behn's " ? This

[1] From the publication (1678) of L'Estrange's version of Marianne Alcoforado's letters to Noel, Marquis de Chamily and St. Leger, *Letters of a Portuguese Nun*, a book often reprinted and one the continued influence of which it is difficult to over-estimate, the amours of nuns, monastery intrigues, and the like in a thousand variants were immensely popular. In 1694 we have *Five Love-Letters written by a Cavalier, in answer to the five love-letters written by a Nun ;* in 1684 *The Amorous A. : or Love in a Nunnery. A novel :* in 1696 Mrs. Manley's *Letters, to which is added a letter from a supposed nun in Portugal to a gentleman in France :* in 1700 *The English Nun ; a comical description of a Nunnery.* Cf. Dryden's *The Assignation, or Love in a Nunnery*, produced 1672, 4to, 1673.

was investigated in detail by Dr. Paul Hamelius of Liège whose *The Source of Southerne's Fatal Marriage* appeared in the *Modern Language Review*, Vol. IV, p. 352 (1909). Hamelius quotes from the memoir [1] in Vol. I of Southerne's works (3 vols.), 1774, " Printed for T. Evans, near York-buildings ; and T. Becket, corner of the Adelphi, Strand." The passage runs : " the plot [of *The Fatal Marriage*] by the author's confession is taken from a novel of Mrs. Behn's called *The Nun ; or, The Fair Vow-Breaker.*" On this he comments : " the ' hint ' of Southerne's own statement was transformed into a confession of borrowing." A little before he also writes : " Among her [Mrs. Behn's] collected novels [2] there is one entitled *The Nun ; or, The Perjur'd Beauty*, and Sir Edmund Gosse has kindly informed me that story is identical with *The Nun ; or, The Fair Vow-Breaker* which appears in the *editio princeps* of 1689 (inaccessible to me)." The critic however is able to discover no analogy betwixt novel and tragedy, nor can the question be adequately solved. He finds that the main business of *The Fatal Marriage* is similar to the theme of *The Virgin Captive*, the fifth story in Roger L'Estrange's *The Spanish Decameron*, published in 1687.[3] Howbeit he draws greater attention to the legend of the lovers of Teruel as dramatized in 1638 by Juan Perez de Montalvan, *Los Amantes de Teruel*,[4] and declares that the likeness between English and Spanish play is quite unmistakable, and that accordingly Southerne must have been acquainted with Spanish. Nevertheless at the end of his article Hamelius confesses " the question is naturally still open whether Southerne was not drawing from some more immediate source—possibly even from some lost version of the story by Mrs. Behn herself," and then again surmises that " In the Dedication Southerne may have merely intended to pay a compliment to his literary friend Mrs. Behn." Aphra [5] Behn had died April 16, 1689, and this last hypothesis is on the face of it extremely improbable.

[1] Written by T. E., who is undoubtedly Evans.

[2] Hamelius uses *All the Histories and Novels* (1705) as being the earliest copy in the British Museum. The first edition of *The Nun ; or, The Perjur'd Beauty* has a separate title page, 1697, and appears bound up in the third edition of *All the Histories and Novels*, general title page 1698.

[3] Advertised in May that year by S. Neale.

[4] There was a comedia on the same subject by A. Reyde Artieda, 1581 ; and yet another the work of Tirso de Molina, 1635, who bases on Artieda.

[5] This is now the accepted form of the name. There are, of course, many variants. See my edition of Mrs. Behn, Vol. I, Memoir, p. xvi.

During the course of my editing Aphra Behn's complete works it naturally became necessary to examine very closely first editions of both plays and novels, not only for the purpose of careful collation but also to transcribe thence the various Prefaces and Epistles Dedicatory (all of great value) which had never been reprinted. Sir Edmund Gosse most generously adding yet another to the many great kindnesses he had shown me, lent me his little duodecimo volume *The History of the Nun ; or, The Fair Vow-Breaker*, Licensed Octob. 22, 1688, Ric. Pocock —Printed for *A. Baskervile*, at the *Bible*, the Corner of *Essex-Street*, against St *Clement's* Church, 1689

It may be noticed that the British Museum is extraordinarily poor in Behn items. Of the novels it only possesses one separate first edition, *The Lucky Mistake*, 1689 : it even wants a copy of the 1683 quarto *The Young King ; or, The Mistake*, a deplorable lacuna.[1] It is of course a matter of common knowledge that the whole Behn bibliography is confused and difficult to an almost unexampled degree.

The History of the Nun ; or, The Fair Vow-Breaker[2] was borrowed from Sir Edmund Gosse's library primarily in order to transcribe the interesting dedication " To The Most Illustrious Princess, The Duchess of Mazarine," but on proceeding to examine the little volume I at once found that here we have an entirely different novel from *The Nun ; or, The Perjur'd Beauty*, and one moreover which has never been collected from the excessively rare original.[3] A second edition appeared in 1698, " London. Printed for Tho. Chapman, at the *Angel* in the *Pall-Mall*." An exemplar exists in the Dyce library, but it is of equal scarcity as the first, if indeed this be not a unique item.

This then is the veritable solution of the whole difficulty and the critics have been most egregiously mistaken. Hamelius' ingenious article is hereby proved to be futile and nugatory.

The story of *The Fair Vow-Breaker* runs as follows : A certain Count Henrick de Vallary (or Valerie) of Iper (Ypres) is so distracted at the death of his wife whom he dearly loves that he joins the Society of Jesus and hands over his infant daughter, Isabella, to the care of her aunt, the abbess of an Augustinian

[1] This was written in 1916.
[2] Miss Charlotte E. Morgan (p. 83) wrongly writes *the Faire Vow-Breaker*.
[3] The book once belonged to Charles Kirkpatrick S[harpe], and has the following note in his hand : " The tragedy of ' the Fatal Marriage ' was suggested by this Novel, not printed in the collection of Madam Aphra's works."

convent. Isabella, as she grows up, resolves to take the veil and in spite of her aunt's wise cautions and her father's warnings persists in this decision. Her wit and beauty are so remarkable that she is already beloved of many gallants, but by none more dearly than Villenoys, who consumed with passion lingers long at Ypres whilst on his way to the siege of Candia. Once however she has pronounced her vows Villenoys betakes himself to the war, and we learn that he is fighting at Candia against the Moslem hordes. Meanwhile Isabella has fallen in love with the brother of a fellow nun, the son of a wealthy noble named Vanhenault. After some languishing and intriguing she escapes from the cloister and the amorous couple fly together to a town forty miles and more away in German territory, where changing their names to Beroone, they are forthwith married and drive "a Farming Trade." The Margrave Vanhenault promptly disinherits his son, and ill luck dogs their footsteps, but after two years " by the Solicitations of the Lady Abbess and the Bishop, who was her near kinsman, they got a Pardon for Isabella's quitting the Monastery and marrying, so that she might now return to her own Country again." Henault's (Beroone's) father however refuses to forgive him unless he will join the French army against the Turks then at Candia, which eventually the unhappy husband is forced to do. Here he meets with Villenoys whom he has known of old. They exchange confidences. In a skirmish Villenoys sees his friend fall and communicates the news to Isabella. When Candia is taken Villenoys returns home and proceeds to woo the widow who is sincerely lamenting the loss of her beloved husband for whose sake she sacrificed so much. After three years he wins her hand, and being a man of the highest position and great affluence they pass five years of tranquil happiness and content. Isabella none the less leads as retired a life as is convenient with her state, and on one occasion when her husband is away for a week hunting she is supping very privately in her own chamber attended but by a maid, Maria. There is a knock at the gate, and Maria answering the summons finds an ill-favoured fellow in an odd habit who delivers her a ring to hand to her mistress. At the sight of the jewel Isabella almost swoons with fear as it is none other than a pledge she had long ago given Henault, who is indeed the mysterious visitor. She greets him, they sup together, and she has a bed made up for him in an adjoining room. Retiring thither he falls asleep. Isabella, whose love for Henault is dead, overcome with shame and agony at the thought of losing wealth, husband, happiness, in a frenzy smothers her visitor ere he can wake, but at that moment Villenoys, whose friend has been taken ill, returns, and instantly notices her horror and confusion. She tells him that Henault has come back, but that when she revealed her second marriage he expired instantly of a broken heart. To save her honour Villenoys places the body in a sack purposing to throw it into the river. But Isabella, fearing that he will reproach her and even perchance reveal her horrid secret, as she is helping to hoist the burden on to his back, desperately sews the sack to his coat with several strong stitches so that when Villenoys with a sudden jerk swings the corpse over the rail of the bridge he himself is dragged down into the water and drowned. The crime is discovered, but Isabella evades all suspicion until the arrival of a French gentleman, who had been a fellow slave with Henault in Turkey, and who having escaped seeks his friend. Questions are asked, and Isabella, brought to justice, confesses all. She is executed, and on the scaffold makes a speech warning all Vow-Breakers.

It is worth while giving a synopsis of so rare a book, and thence it may be clearly seen that the points of resemblance between the novel and tragedy are many and very close. We have the heroine's name Isabella; in the play Biron her first husband has been disinherited by his father Count Baldwin upon his marrying Isabella, who broke out of her convent for his sake, and he has been forced "to go to the Siege of *Candy*, where he was kill'd." Both in novel and play Isabella has obtained the Church's forgiveness for her violated vows. Southerne has Villeroy as the name of Isabella's second husband; Mrs. Behn Villenoys. Biron and Beroone are of course the same word. Both in novel and play the slavery lasts seven years: the incidents of the return and the ring are exactly similar: in Act V, Sc. 2 Isabella frantic is about to stab Biron as he sleeps on a couch, but when he rises she shrieks and throws her poniard away; Mrs. Behn makes her go "to the bed of the unfortunate Henault with a penknife in her hand; but considering, she knew not how to conceal the blood should she cut his throat, she resolves to strangle him." Southerne's catastrophe is of course entirely different from that of the novel. His heroine is innocent throughout and wins all our sympathies. He has also with true dramatic instinct introduced the sinister figure of Carlos, whose treacheries and villainy bring about all the mischiefs, death and woe. Nevertheless many a touch and minute detail in addition to those particularized above are drawn from *The Fair Vow-Breaker*, and by the identification of this novel as a separate piece not as *editio princeps* of *The Perjur'd Beauty* the whole difficulty has been solved, and the source of *The Fatal Marriage* amply revealed. Both *The Nun ; or, The Fair Vow-Breaker* and *The Nun ; or, The Perjur'd Beauty* have of course found their rightful place in my recent edition of Mrs. Behn (Vol. V, The Novels).

Scenes of the amusing underplot of *The Fatal Marriage* (which contains some capital comedy, played as excellently well by Anne Bracegirdle as were the more serious passages by the " famous Madam Barry ") Southerne directly took from *The Night Walker ; or, The Little Thief*, that admirable piece printed as Fletcher's in 1640, having been, according to Herbert's license, " corrected by Shirley " in 1633. The purgatorial farce may be traced to the *Decamerone*, Gior. III, Novella 8, whose rubric runs : " Ferondo, mangiata certa polvere, è sotterrato per morto ; e dall' abate, che la moglie di lui si gode, tratto dalla sepoltura, è messo in prigione, e fattogli credere, che egli è in purgatório ; e poi risuscitato per suo nutrica un figliuolo dello abate, nella moglie di lui generato." It is the *Feronde, ou le Purgatoire* of La Fontaine.

It may not be entirely irrelevant to say a word in favour of Southerne's comic talents, which were certainly of a very high order. The underplot of *The Fatal Marriage* and more particularly that of *Oroonoko*, both almost universally decried, and in later years shockingly mutilated in representation, are first-rate comedy. *The Maid's Last Prayer* and *The Wives' Excuse*, which latter won an immortal compliment from Dryden, have much wit and facile diction, whilst *Sir Antony Love ; or, The Rambling Lady* is replete with spirit, sparkle, and abandon, and equal to the raciest scenes of Vanbrugh and Farquhar themselves.

MYSTICAL SUBSTITUTION

MYSTICAL SUBSTITUTION

IT has been more than once noted by spiritual writers and esoteric thinkers that amongst all the myriad experiences and phenomena of that vast and wonderful science we term Mysticism, there is one law which has, it would seem, in no small degree escaped the attention due to it from the student and the scholar. We mean the law of Mystical Substitution. None the less " cette substitution d'une âme forte débarrassant celle qui ne l'est point, de ses périls et de ses craintes, est une des grandes règles de la Mystique." And there are two reasons, one subtly specious but mistaken, the other deeply significant and true, why there should be this apparent neglect. Mystical substitution, the stretching forth a helping hand, the voluntary assuming to oneself the psychic aridity, the inertia, the temptations, the interior pains and sorrow of those who are fainting by the wayside as it were, who are yielding more and more under the burden which is about to crush them to the dust, is often affirmed to be the peculiar prerogative of the contemplative and cloistered, a task only to be undertaken by mystics who have reached a very high state of progress and perfection, that is to say, who are far in the way of Divine Union. And so to enter the lists to help a brother or a sister in bitter anguish and travail, weary and oppressed to death it may be, is often regarded as the exclusive office of the anchoress, the Poor Clare, enclosed Dominicans, Servites of the Second Order, Carmelites, who by their prayers, penance and vigils may take upon themselves, and so relieve the suffering of those unable to endure it with impunity. There are accordingly many mystics of to-day—I speak of men and women outwardly leading just ordinary commonplace lives—who never dream that for them there lies to hand work in this direction, incalculably valuable and entirely practical. Doubtless some, whilst fully allowing the claim in the case of contemplatives and adepts, will aver that such a work is impossible for themselves, and to a like idea is generally to be traced the common disregard of mystical substitution. Yet, a little careful consideration will show that in varying degrees it is possible for all mystics. Naturally, the neophyte must not expect to compass, must indeed in no circumstances venture to attempt, what is only to be undertaken by those whom we may call the geniuses of Mysticism : the amateur cannot essay the feats of the professional.   And, as will be duly pointed out, considerable danger may sometimes lie in failure.   J. K. Huysmans, who has already been quoted, speaks of " la méthode de substitution qui fut et qui est encore la glorieuse raison d'être des cloîtres," and it is confessedly amongst the convents that to-day we may easily find mystical substitution in its highest and most exalted form, in the fullness of its strength and power, but that is not to say (as many would appear to suppose) that it cannot also be in some measure and usefully practised with very real and happy results by those who are quite unable to retire from the press and " busy hum of men," whose avocations are in cities and amongst crowds.   Retirement, it need hardly be insisted, is of course necessary for all mystics just as it is for the scholar.   And those who can withdraw at will from the disturbing influences and flux of the world to quiet places of beauty and refreshment have no small advantage. Yet even if circumstances only permit of occasional and comparatively brief periods of seclusion, there must none the less not unseldom be an interior retirement from disorders and distractions for all who wish to walk the mystic way.

The first reason then, why mystical substitution is commonly ignored, even by those who have ungrudgingly devoted much time and study to Mysticism, lies in the fact that it has been so widely, but so erroneously, thought of as impracticable save under certain very special conditions of life ; and from disregard to actual disbelief was in many cases not a very far step.   It must be acknowledged indeed that not a few writers on Mysticism have little if anything to say upon this phase of their subject, the fact being that knowledge here, unless experimental, is of very small worth.   For just as the great romanticist, Ann Radcliffe, describes in her masterpieces *The Mysteries of Udolpho* and *The Italian* the landscapes of the Alps and the Abruzzi, and depicts with all the glowing colours and tremendous force of her genius scenes she had never visited nor known, so we have writers on Mysticism, whose books take a high rank for literary skill and encyclopædic detail, whose pages are rich with historical information and precise classifications, and yet, as we read, we instinctively feel that the authors have solely an academic knowledge, not actual experience, of the facts and phenomena they so ably marshal and portray. A salient example of this is R. A. Vaughan, whose *Hours with the Mystics* is often quite frankly unsympathetic, but there are many other writers of more recent date, nay, of the present hour, who probably do not even themselves recognize that fundamentally their interest in Mysticism is that of scholiasts and commentators, that they are not "practising mystics" so to speak. Indeed, far from the slightest apperception of such a fact they must sincerely imagine themselves to be well exercised in Mysticism. For they describe, often with wonderful accuracy and exactness, advanced states and phases of the mystical life, but their lore is too often gleaned from the written word of the mystics and saints; their knowledge exterior and unfelt. The simple shepherds were privileged to worship at Bethlehem before the Wise Men. Notwithstanding then their array of mystical learning, their close familiarity with the pages of Ruysbroeck, S. Teresa, S. John of the Cross, Rolle and the rest, one is often unable to escape the conviction that it is not all thoroughly comprehended and realized. "He who praises the lasciviousness of Alcibiades does not enjoy the pleasure that he had," acutely wrote Count S. C. de Soissons.

It is only to the practising mystic that mystical substitution is of any real value. It is a hidden work, the beginning and the basis of which are love and sympathy: intense sympathy to appreciate and feel for the sufferings of our brothers, be it mental or physical pain; overwelling love to share, if may be, some part of their burden with them. Without these two which walk hand in hand, the work can neither be desired nor begun. Those who have little or no experience in this way will find the first steps slow, but, if undertaken from the true and only motives, inevitably sure. There is nobody, nobody at any rate to whom such a work could make the smallest appeal, who has not some individual, at least one, whose welfare and interests he dearly cherishes, whose love he prizes as a treasure beyond all purchase. At a time such as the present, an hour of obscene chaos, wanton ruin and pitiable woe, when no less gigantic a struggle is in progress than the powers of a diabolical hierarchy striving with all the forces of hell to enslave and dominate the world which we inhabit—at such a time there are thousands of hearts anxious and sick to death for those who are absent and separate, in danger on the battle-field, in peril on the high seas, in agony in the hospital. If love be deep enough, if sympathy be true, it is often possible for those at home mystically to alleviate in some measure the pain and sorrows of those loved, and even to ward off evil from them.   It is well known that in the case of twins a psychic copula binds the two, and when parted by miles of earth and ocean, the illnesses and troubles of the one will, to some degree, find their correspondence and reflection in the other. Love links souls and unites them with this psychic copula.   As Mr. A. E. Waite so admirably insists in his illuminating study *The Way of Divine Union*, Love and Love alone is the " be-all and the end-all " of the mystic's work, thought and being.   And so the lover becomes truly sympathetic ($\sigma\nu\mu\pi\alpha\theta\acute{\eta}s$, affected by like feelings ; suffering with) with the Beloved.

" Tantôt, cette suppléance est purement spirituelle, et tantôt, au contraire, elle n'est adressé qu'aux maladies du corps."   In either case the means of mystical substitution, the method by which it is effected, will seem at first sight extraordinarily simple. They may be summed up in the words—prayer and oblation. But in this prayer there must be an intense concentration of the energies, a recollection, an apprehension of the aim, a yearning and a thirst to help and to share, an intensity and fervour, a mystic wrestling, as it were, with God, even as Israel strove with the Angel, a crying, " Non dimittam te, nisi benedixeris mihi." No tepidity, no impatience, no mere formula of words, no conventionalism must mar that prayer.   It has been pertinently said, " Prayer is the hardest of hard work."   And then, when the offering has been once made, when the mystic with complete unselfishness has asked that he may share and help to bear the burthen, be it physical pain or mental anguish, he must allow himself to remain passive and inert in the hands of God and await the result.

It may be well to remark that sometimes the offering would seem not to be accepted, perhaps not required, and hence there is no application of it.   If this be patently so—herein he who has made the oblation may judge for himself—he can, if he wish, and if his love and sympathy are equal to the work, offer himself anew for some other intention, and ask to aid by mystical substitution any who are in sore stress, naming no name, not knowing whom he comforts.

In the case of those who have not before attempted this

experience it is hard to formulate any general suggestions. But they may be strongly urged at first to direct their intention to the alleviation of only less keen forms of suffering. It must always be remembered that mystical substitution is an ordeal for which considerable firmness and self-reliance are demanded, that the psychic distress the mystic invites, if not borne calmly and with high fortitude, not only defeats its own end but can entail terrible perplexity to himself. It were ill for the neophyte to hazard presumptuously and ignorantly a harder task than he is able to accomplish, and here we have the weighty reason why many mystics have been loath to dwell upon this experience, and have indeed shrunk from reference to it. The late Monsignor Benson tells a tale in *The Mirror of Shalott* which shows the dark consequences that may ensue from this mystic immolation; a tale which, if fictional in presentation, is true in fact. The great safeguard against such peril, against failure, is Love.

Frequently one of the first signs of the efficacy of mystical substitution is that the person who has made the offering is flooded with intense mental depression, and this without any apparent or traceable cause. If he is not able to accept the initial ordeal willingly and gladly, to cope with it bravely and well, if he cannot continue his daily tasks with precision and accuracy, cannot persevere in his interior life, his devotions, meditation, reading (albeit the sap and savour of these is gone), it will show that either he has sought too heavy a burden, or else, what is the more likely, that he is altogether unready for the experience, which should be forthwith abandoned.

The oblations of many heroic souls self-immolated in this mystical way on the altar of love and sympathy have been recorded, but often they seem histories written for our admiration rather than our imitation. Yet it is well to remember that even the greatest and most noble began with little things, proving their strength, and advanced step by step along a path which is open to all who desire, who love. Thus, to mention only a very few names—S. Teresa took upon herself and bore without flinching the temptations of a priest well-nigh driven to despair. Blessed Mary Bartholomaea Bagnesi, a Dominican, was noted throughout Florence in the sixteenth century for relieving, by taking upon herself, the illnesses and troubles of her neighbours and of the wretched who had recourse to her. She became a complete invalid, and died, a victim to love, in 1577. Anna

Maria Taigi, the Roman matron, who was perhaps the most illumined seer of the nineteenth century, often bore the sufferings both interior and physical of those who sought her aid. So Soeur Bernard de la Croix, who died in 1847, and Barbara of S. Dominic, a Spanish votary, who offered her life in 1872 for the cure of a sister nun long confined to her bed by a complication of agonizing disorders, were both wont to take upon their shoulders the mental anguish and miseries of others. But mystical substitution must not be thought a mere exotic of the cloister. There are many instances of the same thing happening all around us to-day, only, as will be well understood, most of these cases are so intimate they cannot for that and other obvious reasons be detailed here.

Yet, it may be worth while mentioning one pertinent experience, not as in any way indeed comparable with those of the ecstatics and mystics we have named, but rather as showing the possibility of substitution and kindred phases of practical mysticism amongst perfectly ordinary people in commonplace circumstances. It is well known that many houses of contemplatives devote the days of the Carnival to special prayer, meditation and spiritual exercises, counterbalancing in some wise the gluttony, revelry, and riot of that wanton season which often seems a very apogee of materialism and empty follies, opportune moments for man's worst passions. Nowhere perhaps is this more in evidence than along the Riviera, nowhere is the Carnival so extravagant and reckless as in Nice, Mentone, and in Monaco, " where the witch holds her high court and never-ending festival of sin in the painted banquet-halls and among the green tables." And so it is the annual custom of the Carmelites in their sunny little convent at San Remo to pass these days in even yet stricter discipline than is their wont, an expiation and compensation for the saturnalia of those wine-stained hours. Some years ago a number of visitors, not more than a dozen all told, who had become friendly owing to their mutual interest in Mysticism, felt impelled to join the nuns in their work. A simple rule of life for those few days was laid down, details being left to the individual, but all combined and co-operated to concentrate thought and activities upon a higher plane counter to the revellers who appear to delight in sinking to buffooneries that are certainly unbecoming if not entirely degrading. The psychic experiences of the mystics were very remarkable. Amongst other things all suffered during the time of their oblation from intense mental lassitude and a spiritual aridity which are always accounted sure proofs that the substitution has been accepted and prevails. It may further be noted that this psychological state began abruptly in each case immediately the oblation had been made, the interior disorders and pain increased almost hourly, and no relief nor waning was found until the dark cloud dispersed suddenly, in a moment, to be succeeded by the sunshine of an interior peace, and consolations which were all the sweeter from their contrast with the preceding desolation.

Inadequately enough and briefly we have endeavoured to review and draw attention to a phase of Mysticism which, although it has its own peculiar difficulties, has also its peculiar profit and rewards. And not the least of these must be the knowledge that we are aiding in a very true and vital way those whom we love. Mystical substitution is, after all, but an extension of thought, of prayer, a realization. It is a shadow of the great Unitive Life.

S. CATHERINE OF SIENA

S. CATHERINE OF SIENA

DISMISSED with half-a-dozen lines and a scornful note by Dean Milman in his *History of Latin Christianity*, S. Catherine of Siena is nevertheless one of the grandest and most striking figures in those turbid times, when the mediæval sky was about to be faintly tinged by the grey light herald of the Renaissance dawn. For certes it is an extraordinary fact indeed that a poor nun, without wealth, without learning, without beauty, should have attained in those ages of unbridled lust and bloodshed to an ideal of saintliness which canonized her yet living in a people's heart, and at the same time have been crowned with diplomatic honours, interposing in an hour when all things seemed trebly confounded between " Pope, Prince, and Republic," and, by her influence and word, bringing to a successful issue crises which affected the destiny of Christendom.

If, as modern science tells us, it be unquestionably true that every effect invariably betokens and implies an adequate cause, surely it will not be lost labour briefly to inquire how it came about that in the middle of the fourteenth century, amid scenes of shameless profligacy and lawlessness, amid horrors of blood and crime almost unparalleled in history, this Dominican nun executed the most delicate negotiations, toiled amongst men stricken of pestilence, swayed furious and maddened mobs, harangued councils of prelates and nobles, corresponded with queens and cardinals, and directed the actions of the Pope himself.

S. Catherine was the youngest of very many children born to Jacopo and Lapa Benincasa, Sienese citizens. Her father exercised the trades of dyer and fuller, and in the year of her birth, 1347, Siena had reached the climax of prosperity and power, rivalling even Florence in wealth and splendour. But at the hour of her greatest exaltation the city was brought low. The plague suddenly began its awful ravages, and ere long swept off 80,000 of her sons.

In the midst of such calamities Catherine grew up almost unnoticed, but even so it was remarked that she was unlike her girl companions. At seven years old she longed for a cloistral life, and saw visions. One eventide as she sat with her young brother near a fountain outside the city walls, it seemed to her that the heavens opened, and she beheld Christ upon a throne, with S. Peter, S. Paul, and S. John the Divine. While she gazed, oblivious of all else, her brother shook her to recall her to herself. She turned to him, but when she looked up again the wondrous sight had vanished : with a bitter cry she throws herself upon the ground and weeps piteously. So she grew to girlhood, living apart, solitary and imaginative, ever dreaming of things beyond the veil, a most fervid mystic, intensely realizing in her own life what other souls as ardent, but less ecstatic, deem mere poetic raptures. She remembered the legend of her patroness, S. Catherine of Alexandria, the bride of Christ, and she prayed to the Blessed Mother of God that she would bestow her Divine Son upon her also. Madonna granted her prayer, and linked her hand with that of Christ, and from thenceforth did Catherine vow a vow of perpetual chastity. She was the spouse of God.

In consequence of this she persisted in refusing the proposals made by her parents that she should wed. To them, her vigils, her ecstasies, her penances and fasting seemed vain folly. But Catherine rejected all suitors. At length her parents, excited to anger, imposed upon her the most servile duties of the household. Nothing was too mean or too hard for her to undertake. She patiently fulfilled every task with unwearying obedience, until finally her father and mother gave way and consented to her becoming a religious. At the age of sixteen she entered the Dominican Order. Then followed a period of most rigid discipline. For three long years she never quitted her cell but to enter the church. Maintaining a silence unbroken save to her confessor alone, sleeping but two hours, laid stretched upon the cold earth, eating only vegetables and a morsel of bread, ruthlessly scourging her tender body, ever clad in roughest sackcloth, she became emaciated, worn by spiritual conflicts and temptations, half delirious with the tension of long ecstasies.

We are told that her torments were terrible. The tempter ever lurked at her ear, filling her soul with the vilest imaginings, seeking to win her from the path of perfection ; but at midnight she would arise to scourge herself till the blood streamed from her anguished frame. She lay prostrate on the chilly flags before the altar, calling upon her Bridegroom to help her; and He comforted her with His visible presence. He paced the chapel with her, talking of peace and ineffable love, until she swooned in raptures of supersensual communion.

Thus she related, thus she believed, and thus it was. We must not confound S. Catherine with those miserable shams and their sickly hysterics, alas! too common in every age. The reality of her inspirations and her genius are amply proven by her warm sympathy, her moral dignity, and the great practical work which she did in the world. Those were times of sublimest faith. Heaven lay around them in that holy infancy. Metaphors became to S. Catherine actual and true in a most real sense. Wrapt in penance and prayer she literally interpreted vivid parabolas.

One morning, on the fourth Sunday of Lent, *Laetare*, 1375, when meditating at early dawn in the chapel of S. Cristina, at Pisa, before a crucifix much venerated for its antiquity, S. Catherine, being absorbed in devotion, saw the Sacred Wounds stream with blood; five crimson rays of light smote her side, her hands, and feet. She was rent in awful throes, and, awaking from her trance, she cried to Raymond of Capua, her confessor: " Behold! I bear in my body the marks of the Lord Jesus! " O marvellous girl enthusiast! She desired to be literally " crucified with Christ," not satisfied with sentiment and simile, she burned for the absolute satisfaction of her desire. Was it not just that the bride should share the sorrows of her Lord?

This miracle had happened before to S. Francis of Assisi. These souls of heroic mould could ill endure the trammels of a body, and soared to heights to which we dare not aspire. With reverence let us turn away our giddy eyes, nor seek to explain their raptures of love, their enthusiasms and profoundest ecstasies.

It is obvious, however, that in many cases a temperament like S. Catherine's has led to the grossest abuse. Weak, hysterical women and fanatical men, without possessing a tithe of her abilities, and totally misunderstanding her communion with heavenly things, have obtained an ephemeral reputation for holiness by indulging in the wildest phantoms of a disordered brain. It is evident that the frenzies of would-be saints have often annihilated intellectual vigour and encouraged the idlest superstition; but the marvellous visions of S. Catherine were proper to her time and country. They inspired her with unbounded devotion and love, they supported her through all the stress of a busy life.   This inner life was, as it were, her stay, the fount from whence she drew when wearied with the quarrels of pontiff and princes, the dissensions of city and province.

It is no part of our theme to detail her political experiences and to show a maiden of twenty-nine going forth to arrange terms with the Pope at Avignon ; and she is successful beyond belief.   The Pope commits himself wholly to her directions, the court of Cardinals desire nothing but her will.   John XXII, a Frenchman, had taken up his residence at Avignon, and since then that city had become the Pontiff's abode.   Rome left desolate and widowed is almost given over to utter destruction. Christendom is divided, and monarchs incline some this way, some that.   A dreadful crisis seems impending, which will perhaps involve the western world in helpless anarchy and ruin. The root of the mischief was the abandonment of Rome ; and so at the word of the Sienese nun, Pope Gregory XI agrees to return thither, sending her on in advance to Genoa, where she meets him, and together they enter the Eternal City.

Ah ! yes, and then she retires to her cell once more to resume her mystic life, once more to take up the broken thread of prayer and penance, to fast, to watch, to weep ; and there she lives protectress of her dear Siena, teaching the little children who love to cluster round her knees, visiting the poor, tending the sick, preaching love and peace to all.

Her personal influence was immense.   Crowds thronged to hear her speak, and those who could not draw near enough to catch the words that fell from her lips remained afar off, gazing at her face, radiant with holiness and purity.   Enemies were reconciled, the vendetta became a thing unknown, law suits were settled by her word, all strife seemed quelled by her addresses.

We yet possess several of her writings.   "Doctrina eius infusa, non acquisita fuit," says the Breviary.   The *Dialogue*, so suave and unctuous, so illuminating, so divinely inspired, is no series of futile and incoherent rhapsodies, but a masterful treatise upon the spiritual life.   It is mainly concerned with the communion of a soul with God, and in spite of much that is novel, and to some perhaps even bizarre, it is a work of great value, often with deep thoughts and sternest moral teaching underlying apparently mere ecstatic exclamations.   Love is her creed.   The constant repetition of this word throughout her writings is most striking. When dwelling upon her mystical wedlock she cries, " O blood ! O fire ! O ineffable love ! " Or again in a prayer, which is yet used by the people of Siena, she writes, " O Spirito Santo, O Deita eterna, Cristo Amore ! O amore ineffable ! Infiammami del tuo dulcissimo amore. Cristo amore. Cristo amore ! "

One incident in particular which S. Catherine relates in a letter to Raymond of Capua shows her character in an exquisitely beautiful light. Nicola Tuldo, a citizen of Perugia, had been condemned to death for treason. This youth, full of the hot joy of the world's green spring, abandoned himself to utter despair. Revolting against the sentence he refused all consolation, and drove with curses from his cell the priests who ventured to approach him. Then Catherine visited him, " whence," she writes, " he received such comfort that he confessed, and made me promise by the love of God to stand at the block beside him on the day of his execution." Sublime in her spotless sanctity and sisterly love she brought peace and hope to the soul of this hapless youth. Perchance he had never known a pure love in all his riotous life, and when the gracious Catherine appeared the mask of cynicism was rent aside and his heart went out to her in chivalrous devotion.

Long time she stayed with him, laying his head upon her breast and soothing him as a frightened child. Upon the morning of the day of his execution they communicated together. His only cry was, " Lady, remain with me, and it shall be well, I die content." When the hour came she, who herself so greatly yearned for the red rose of martyrdom, stood beside him upon the scaffold holding his hands until she forgot the place, the crowd, the awful preparations, and prayed aloud for his soul. Then she placed his head upon the block and comforted him. The last word he uttered was her name. The axe fell, and Catherine beheld his soul borne aloft by angels into the highest heaven. When she arose from her trance, the severed head lay in her hands and her dress was saturated with blood which she could scarcely bear to wash away, so greatly did she triumph in the soul she had saved.

O depths of love unfathomable ! Love is the keynote of her life as it is of the lives of all those profound, almost superhuman and yet withal so intensely human, beings we know full well.

Love transfixes and permeates them every one, whether it be S. Francis upon the Umbrian hills carolling to his little sisters the birds, or S. Rose tending her garden of sweet-scented flowers, or S. Elizabeth pressing to her bosom the miraculous blossoms as she hastes down the Wartburg, or S. Antony fondling the Infant Christ. 'Tis these things which linger in our hearts when the austerities of a S. Bruno and the mortifications of a S. Bernard are forgotten, or else but remembered as deep shadows in the picture.

Love, warm human love, is the one great explanation of much in the life of S. Catherine, and many another saint, that would else seem to us fantastic and unreal. It is this adorant passion transcending all carnal bonds that is the cause of wonderful phenomena in the higher mysticism, phenomena which make many smile, but which have again and again been renewed and most unmistakably verified in quite recent years.[1] S. Catherine Adorni of Genoa dipped her hands in icy water and it boiled; snow melted around S. Peter of Alcantara; Venerable Ursula Benicasa, foundress of the Theatine nuns, was consumed with so fierce a flame that at times smoke issued from her mouth.

However it may be noted that in all her miracles and visions S. Catherine of Siena presents us with no unique experience. Her namesake of Alexandria had already been termed the spouse of Christ, and had been regarded as mystically betrothed to Him. S. Francis had received the stigmata. Her ecstasies, her raptures, had all been vouchsafed to other saints. Numerous passages in her *Dialogue* might be paralleled in kindred works : in the Book of the Visions of the Blessed Angela of Foligno, in the writings of S. Maria Maddalena de Pazzi, and many more. It is for her womanhood that we admire her so singly, for that graciousness and tenderness which bowed hearts before her, for her unselfish and gentle life, leaving behind it a sweetness and loveliness often lacking in the lives of many a saint of excelling power and cast in a sterner mould.

S. Catherine died at Rome on 29 April, 1380, in her thirty-third year. Spent with fasting and want of sleep, her frame torn

---

[1] Linen scorched by the fire of the heart was observed on the stigmatized Palma-Maria Matanelli by Dr. Imbert-Gourbeyre, who investigated the case most carefully, and who asserts that there is much in the phenomena of mysticism quite inexplicable by modern science. Many other cases of a similar nature which have been the subject of scientific investigation might be cited.

and wasted by thong and mortification, exhausted by the tension of almost continuous visions and exaltations, surrounded by a circle of weeping enthusiasts, she closed her weary eyes murmuring " The Glory of God." And then she fell asleep.

Not only does there exist an authentic portrait of the Saint, but in the Church of San Domenico at Siena is preserved her head embalmed immediately after death. As to the genuineness of this relic there can be no doubt. Every particular and incident of her life was recorded by devoted contemporaries. Her veil and staff, her enamelled vinaigrette, the bag in which she collected alms, her lantern used to visit the sick at night, all these are treasured in the church.

30 April is the principal Festa of the Saint.[1] All Siena keeps holiday upon the feast of " Our Most Holy and Seraphic Mother Catherine." Processions of priests and acolytes and pious confraternities holding innumerable tapers, and little girls dressed all in white, parade the city bearing an immense silver image of their patroness. Censers and banners and crosses go in front, then follow the relics beneath a canopy, rose leaves and flowers are scattered in the path. All is life and gaiety in the bustling streets. San Domenico, too, is thronged with a surging multitude. The faithful are kneeling before the Saint's shrine, which blazes with radiance of light. The music at the high altar mingles with the multiplied nasal drone of Tuscan priests ; for masses are continually said at every altar from earliest dawn. And there, far above all, in the glare of Italian sunlight and myriad candles, behind the baroque painting and tawdry gilding of a much-bedecked shrine, looks out the pale, dead, white face which spoke and suffered so much six long centuries ago.

[1] The Feast of the Espousals with Jesus is kept on the Thursday before Quinquagesima Sunday ; the Feast of the Holy Stigmata on 3 April.

S. ANTONY OF PADUA

S. ANTONY OF PADUA

SUCH is the tender sweetness and sympathy, such the never-fading beauty of "the eldest son of S. Francis" as S. Antony of Padua has been called, that a world which in its desperate earnestness about mere material things has well-nigh forgotten the mystic enthusiasms of the saints, can still find a few moments now and again to turn confidingly to him who was so lovely in his life, and who even in these late days is yet so swift in his answer to prayer, so compassionate and pitiful, that hard and barren indeed are the hearts unmoved by his grace, nor throughout all Catholic Christendom is there scarce a sanctuary, be it noble minster and soaring cathedral or humble village church and poor cloister chapel, where we may not kneel before the barefoot brown friar with his book, his white lilies, and the blazing flame that typifies his ardent soul.

Born in 1195 at Lisbon, the son of a distinguished officer, Martin de Bullones, S. Antony received at his baptism the name of Ferdinand, which, when he became a Franciscan, he changed to that of Antony, out of devotion, it is said, to the famous cenobite Antony, the founder of Monachism. The boy had his schooling from the canons of the cathedral of Lisbon, but at the age of fifteen he "entered among the regular canons of S. Austin," and eight years later, already far on the way of perfection and desiring greater seclusion, he withdrew to the lonely convent of Holy Rood at Coimbra. About this time it happened that Dom Pedro, Infante of Portugal, with much pomp and worship brought back from Morocco the relics of five Franciscans, S. Berard and his companions, who preaching the love of Christ had been murdered on the shores of Africa by the fierce native tribes. Nothing would now content Antony but that he also must go forth to lay down his life, first joining that order whose poverty, whose mysticism and utter abnegation so compelled and drew his burning heart. Accordingly, with the consent of his prior, he entered into the Order of Little Poor Men, and straightway set out for Africa. Here, however, he was immediately seized with so severe an illness that he was obliged to re-embark for Spain, but contrary winds drove him to the coast of Italy, and he presently arrived at Assisi and saw S. Francis, who was holding a general chapter of the order there. We next find him in seclusion at a hermitage near Bologna, where his celestial communications, his ecstasies and visions, his eloquence and scholarship are not so much as guessed at, until one day the superior obliged him, reluctant though he was, to deliver a discourse to the brethren, and all were astonished at his learning and his power, upon report of which Father Francis himself wrote to his dear son bidding him study and read sacred theology to the friars, adding, however, this commendation : " Be careful that you do not extinguish in yourself, or in them, the spirit of prayer." Under obedience then he taught with universal applause and growing fame at the great universities, at Bologna, Toulouse, Montpelier, Paris and Padua.

But the honours of the schools proved very irksome to his humble soul, and anon he renounced the chair of divinity and philosophy to go forth a wanderer up and down the country-side, travelling over many lands, but chiefly through the distraught and war-wracked provinces of North Italy, exhorting, consoling, comforting, and sharply rebuking ill in high places. Like his Master of old, " he went about doing good." For wheresoever he came he preached Peace, " the peace of justice and the peace of liberty." He was a true Franciscan, a saint of exquisitely poetical imagination. His heart overflowed with the love of nature and the love of his dumb brethren, the animals. The downy whiteness of the swans, the lithe storks and their tender care for their young, the perfume and colour of the flowers of the field, the fragrance of early dawn, the cool and calm of starry night, all these he dwelt on with lingering joy. Of his miracles I will not speak ; do they not continue even to-day ? Many also may be seen pictured around his shrine, painted there by Titian, by Campagnola and Contarini ; whilst Donatello has wrought in immortal bronze the legend of the mule turning aside from the sieve full of oats to kneel before the Saint what time he carried the Blessed Host. In the great picture Murillo made for Seville Cathedral, S. Antony is visited by the infant Christ. It is said that as the Saint was expounding to a crowded congregation the mystery of the Incarnation the form of a Babe Who smiled upon him descended in a flood of dazzling glory

and rested awhile upon his book.   This is perhaps the commonest
and most familiar of all representations of the Saint.

S. Francis, story tells, loved the birds with an overwhelming
love and even preached to them, for in the fullness of his charity
he literally interpreted the text : " Go ye into all the world, and
preach the gospel to every creature." So also S. Antony
preached to the fishes.   On a day when he was at Rimini the
people, being hardened and stiff-necked, gave no heed to his
words, and the Saint went out of the town to a bank betwixt
the river and open sea, and cried aloud : " Hear the word of
God, O ye fishes of the sea and of the river ! " And " forthwith
there came unto him to the bank a multitude of fishes, great
and small and what between . . . and they all held up their
heads above the water and all stood attentive," whereupon the
Saint bade them bless their Creator, who had given them a
clear, translucent element wherein to dwell, both sweet waters
and salt, and food, and fins that they might roam wheresoever
they pleased.   This beautiful legend may be read in the *Fioretti*,
and seen in many a fresco and curious carving of ivory and
stone.

At last S. Antony came face to face with the fiercest and most
cruel of all Italian despots, the blood-maniac Ezzelino da Romano,

Grey, wizened, dwarfish, devil Ecelin.

This bestial monster, who in one day murdered eleven thousand
men in Padua, and, at the capture of Friola, hideously mutilated
the whole population, man, woman, and child, casting them
forth blind and maimed to perish miserably, was obsessed by a
cold, calculating passion for evil and slaughter that could never
be satiated.   But the Saint confronting him without fear or
hesitation very sternly rebuked his sins, whereupon the tyrant,
instead of roughly ordering his *bravi* to strike Antony down,
suddenly descended from his throne, and all pale and trembling
fell suppliant at the feet of the humble friar, promising amend-
ment and begging him to intercede with God for pardon and
mercy.   Under Antony's influence Ezzelino, for a while, entirely
changed his ways, but after the Saint's death he relapsed into
his former crimes, and so at the last perished in despair.   It
has been said that the Saint's rebuke of Ezzelino is equal to all
the miracles together.   Fittingly did Pope Gregory IX hail
Antony as " Ark of the Covenant."   Well may we love him and
kneel before him to-day.

In the last week of May, 1231, Antony, who was then at Padua, fell ill, and in spite of every effort he soon became unable to rise from his poor pallet. On the morning of June 13, he comforted with sweet words his brethren, who stood weeping around, and having greeted each one severally, he began to recite his favourite hymn, " O gloriosa Virginum, Sublimis inter sidera," but even as he spoke the holy words his soul passed to eternity. At the same moment the little children, as if divinely inspired, began to run about the streets of the city, proclaiming aloud, " The Saint is dead! The Saint is dead! " and the bells in the churches, touched by no visible hand, rang out, not a knell of woe but peal upon peal of triumph. Antony was officially canonized before a twelvemonth had passed, and there are perhaps few more gorgeous fanes in Italy than that huge and stately basilica, " Il Santo," as it is locally called, the boast of " many-domed Padua," where lies the body of the meek Franciscan friar. His shrine is splendid beyond all description with coloured marbles and glistening alabaster; it is adorned with bronzes and richest silver-work, aglow with gems and precious stones; before it burn innumerable lamps of gold, and in giant candelabra tall tapers of virgin wax are lighted unceasingly. An endless train of suppliants, each, as the custom is, laying one hand upon the cold malachite and porphyry of the tomb, beseeches the help and patronage of the Saint. Miracles are wrought; his praises are sung by trained choirs of marvellous melody; year by year his great feast (June 13th) is observed with extraordinary solemnity. That day too, in every Franciscan convent and monastery the whole wide world over, fair white lilies are blessed and distributed in honour of S. Antony, the priest praying with exquisite symbolism that whatsoever home and hearth these flowers adorn may be long preserved in health, plenty, purity, and peace.

But whether one is privileged to worship at his glorious sanctuary in Padua, or whether one kneels before some poor plaster image in a tiny chapel at home, S. Antony is none the less swift to hear and ready to aid. The whole world loves him and turns to him when it has lost or mislaid anything, but in comparison that is nothing, for he is one of the greatest spiritual guides who has ever passed beyond, still stretching out helping hands to us, a control who can direct and comfort to-day, can point the road to the highest things and set our feet in the right path. His power in the psychic realm is indeed miraculous, as has been experienced again and again by his clients. The words written of S. Antony by the Seraphic Doctor, Bonaventura, six hundred years ago, ring true as ever : " Si quaeris miracula, mors, error, calamitas, fugiunt . . . resque perditas petunt, et accipiunt juvenes et cani." " If it be that you look for miracles, lo ! death, falsehood, and every woe are vanquished . . . both young and old seek for what is lost, they seek and obtain." And it is not temporal things alone that the Lily of Padua can give us ; ask, and he will give love, charity, peace, happiness, the mystic graces of the spiritual life, which is the only reality.